ECONOMICS

COURSEWORK COMPANION

Keith West

GCSE

Charles Letts & Co Ltd
London, Edinburgh & New York

First published 1989
by Charles Letts & Co Ltd
Diary House, Borough Road, London SE1 1DW

Text: © Keith West 1989

Cover photograph: Michael Rochipp, Image Bank;
Handwriting samples: Artistic License;
Diagrams: Tek Art;
Cartoons: Michael Renouf, Viv Quillin.
© Charles Letts & Co Ltd 1989

British Library Cataloguing in Publication Data

West, Keith
    GCSE economics — (Letts coursework
    companion)
    1. Economics — For schools
    I. Title
    330

ISBN 0 85097 859 9

Printed and bound in Great Britain by
Charles Letts (Scotland) Ltd

Contents

SECTION ONE

What is coursework?

The general purpose of coursework is to enable you to show what you **know**, what you **understand** and what you can **do**. It provides opportunities to carry out research outside of the classroom. You can refer to books, newspapers and other people for information. You do not have to rely solely on your memory as you would in a formal examination.

Important **skills** (or **abilities**) other than memory are being assessed in coursework. The main abilities are:

1 Collection and use of information
2 Presentation of data
3 Application of knowledge
4 Analysis of data
5 Evaluation of evidence

The percentage of the total assessment given for each skill varies between the different examination groups' syllabuses. In certain syllabuses some of the skills are combined and assessed jointly. Occasionally they are expressed slightly differently, as explained in Section Two (Syllabus analysis).

Levels of performance

For each skill, various levels of performance can be identified. These levels can be approximately linked to GCSE gradings, as follows:

Level of performance	Likely GCSE grade
Minimum	G, F
Average	E, D
Good	C
Excellent	B, A

Each level of performance for each skill will be marked over a certain range. For instance, if information gathering is marked out of 10, then 8 to 10 marks may represent excellent performance, with 8 marks meriting a GCSE grade B and 10 marks indicating a GCSE grade A standard.

Table 1.1 describes the various levels of performance for each skill. The easiest skill is at the top and the minimum level of performance is on the left. You should be aiming at the excellent column in each case.

Assessment of coursework

You must hand in something for every coursework assignment. If you do not finish an assignment by the deadline date, give in what you have done. This can obtain you some marks. Similarly, if two assignments are required for your final submission and you have only done one, still submit it – your maximum possible mark for coursework will be halved, but you will still qualify for a final grade. Anyone who does not submit any coursework will not get a final grade, no matter what they achieve in the examination. They will receive a 'NO RESULT' certificate. This is worse than a grade 'G' which is the lowest pass grade.

Skill	Level of performance			
	Minimum	Average	Good	Excellent
Information gathering	Some information collected but mostly irrelevant	Information mostly relevant but not organized	Information relevant and soundly organized	Information relevant, clearly explained and carefully organized
Presentation	Some headings but very little planning and presentation	Appropriate structure but few different presentational techniques	Formal and logical structure with appropriate presentation	Formal and logical structure with data clearly presented using a range of techniques
Application	Some information which is relevant but no use of economic concepts	Appropriate use of information but little application of economic concepts	Some application of economic concepts to relevant information	Thorough understanding and use of many economic concepts
Analysis	Data considered but rather simply, briefly and generally	Data selected and broken into sections for interpretation but a tendency to generalize	Data carefully selected and clearly understood but interpretation sometimes superficial	Accurate, relevant and thoughtful interpretation of data
Evaluation	A few judgments but rather simple	A conclusion attempted but with limited reasoning	An organized conclusion with some examination of arguments and opinions	A well-organized and clearly explained conclusion with a recognition of research limitations

Table 1.1 Levels of performance for assessment skills

The completed assignment will be initially marked **by your teacher** who will receive guidance from the examination group. As well as receiving guidance material on grading, teachers will also have attended standardizing meetings, where actual assignments are assessed by many teachers and standards are established. The **Chief Moderator** is responsible for setting these standards.

After your assignment has been marked, it will be **moderated**. Although the procedures and numbers vary slightly between examination groups, there is a common approach. Each school, or **centre**, has to assess the work of all of its candidates. If there are several groups in your school studying Economics for GCSE, the school will hold its own standardizing meeting, so that different teachers' marking comes into line. Then a **sample** of the centre's work will be sent to an **assistant moderator**, who has been trained by the Chief Moderator. The assistant moderator will confirm the standards or recommend adjustments to the centre's marks.

The assignment marks are eventually combined with the examination marks to give a final grade, which is usually received in late August. After your results are announced, most boards allow you to obtain your assignment to keep (forever if you wish!). The date when assignments become available varies slightly between examination groups, but it is usually not later than 31 October.

Syllabus analysis

Your syllabus

It is unwise to begin any work before you know what you are expected to achieve. For your GCSE courses 'what you are expected to achieve' is set out in the course **syllabus**. It is important that you obtain a copy of your syllabus. Your teacher may be able to provide you with one. If this is not possible you should write to your exam board. A list of addresses is given in Appendix 1. Which board you should write to depends on what area of the country you are in. If you are not sure which board to write to, check with your teacher.

Analysing the syllabus

When you have a copy of the syllabus the first thing to find out is which skills are tested. These are briefly outlined in the 'syllabus analysis' section of the syllabus. You will also be able to discover the importance of each skill in the overall assessment. The marks (percentages) shown for each skill will indicate its relative importance.

A summary of the syllabus analyses (except Scotland) is given in Appendix 1. It may be useful to refer to this when reading the following notes.

NB The most up-to-date syllabuses available (1990/91) have been used to compile this summary, but you should always try to obtain a copy of *your* syllabus because they may be amended in future years. The syllabus may contain useful information about the subject content of your course, as well as about assessment.

In some syllabuses you may notice that a specific percentage is not given for each specific skill involved in the coursework. This is because the syllabus either does not use the same terms throughout the syllabus or combines more than one skill together when allotting a certain number of marks.

Most examination groups require at least two assignments of more than 1000 words each. At present the NEA is the only group which allows teachers (and/or students) a choice of the number of assignments to be submitted.

Your teacher may ask you to complete more than the number of assignments required. This will enable you to choose your best ones to submit, at the end of your course.

Generally where several assignments are required a shorter length is expected.

Don't be frightened by the word length which is specified. A 1000 word assignment works out at about 5 pages of A4 paper in average handwriting. Your finished assignment will probably exceed 5 pages because of diagrams, graphs and other non-written elements. It is a good idea to look at examples of completed assignments. Your teacher may have some from previous years to show you and there is a model assignment at the back of this book (Appendix 2).

The comment at the beginning of this section – that it is unwise to start before you know what is expected of you – applies to each assignment as much as to the whole course. If your teacher says something like 'Do a project on banks', politely ask 'What is required?' In particular, you should find out how big the project is expected to be and how long you have to complete it.

✓ Checklist

DO
- get a copy of your syllabus
- find out which skills are tested
- discover the marks awarded for each skill (indicating relative importance)
- read through the levels of performance
- try to see examples of completed assignments
- follow the advice in the rest of this book

DON'T
- start until you know what is expected of you
- rely entirely on the syllabus analysis table given in Appendix 1
- begin an assignment before you know how long it should be and when it is due

Forward planning

The most important message I can give you is **'plan ahead'**. The best assignments are generally those that have been carefully planned. Organizing yourself is vital, if the effort you put into your assignment work is to be worthwhile.

A diary

The most useful tool for forward planning is a diary or calendar. You should put the important deadline dates in the diary and/or on the calendar. Keep it in a handy place, preferably where you do schoolwork at home. An example of a simple calendar is shown overleaf. It covers one project to be completed over eight months.

Starting the diary on 1 April was intentional, not a joke. By that stage you will be at least two terms into your course and have an Easter holiday for initial thinking. Your teacher is unlikely to start you on an assignment any sooner, especially if you have only one assignment to complete, because you will not have been introduced to enough of the concepts and themes of Economics before then.

If you are required to produce three assignments, the time period will be significantly reduced. However, don't worry – you will not be expected to do as detailed an assignment as the one illustrated above.

When planning your deadlines for an assignment, it is important to build some **slack** into your plan. You should fix yourself a **personal deadline** in advance of the official one (set by your teacher). At least **two weeks' leeway** is advised. This will enable you to cope with any unexpected problems which might arise, being ill, your teacher being away, mislaying your folder, survey sheets not being returned, etc.

You will probably be doing other GCSE subjects besides Economics. You will have coursework assignments for them too. By using a diary to spread the work of each assignment as shown in the example above, you should be able to avoid overloads, e.g. having more than one assignment to complete in the same weekend. If such a clash looks unavoidable, discuss it with your subject teachers. They may be able to help you reorganize your schedule to avoid the problem. If lots of students are similarly affected they may consider changing their deadlines. Remember, they cannot help if they don't know that you have a problem.

Folders

Keep a separate folder or file for each assignment in each subject. Try to use the envelope-style files so that it is less likely that you will lose things. Using a different-coloured folder for each subject and/or assignment is also useful. This is so that you do not pick up the wrong one to take to school, if you are working on the assignment in class. Also, so that you put any notes, clippings, etc in the correct folder – as a moderator, I have occasionally found an assignment with material from other subjects in it! If you keep all your assignment folders together in a set place you will be less likely to lose one.

Example

	Week beginning	Work to be completed
April	1	
	8	
	15	
	22	
	29	
May	6	
	13	
	20	
	27	
June	3	
	10	Collection of background information
	17	
	24	
July	1	
	8	
	15	
	22	Overall plan submitted
	29	
August	5	
	12	Preliminary writing
	19	
	26	
September	2	
	9	Introduction written
	16	
	23	Preparations for survey
	30	
October	7	
	14	Survey questions devised
	21	
	28	Survey questions duplicated
November	4	
	11	Data collection and analysis
	18	
	25	
December	2	
	9	Analysis completed
	16	
	23	All material collated and organized
	30	
January	6	
	13	
	20	Final version written
	27	
February	3	
	10	Teacher's completion deadline
	17	
	24	
March	3	
	10	
	17	
	24	
	31	Exam Board final deadline

Writing and rewriting

Do not expect to produce a perfect project straight off. You should not be surprised if your (carefully made) plans need to be modified along the way or if your early work needs to be rewritten or rearranged. These are common problems with all research at any level, so stay calm! You must accept that you may need to **re-order** and **re-write** what at first seemed to be 'good stuff'.

Because future changes are likely, you should:

1 Write on file paper so that the order of material can be altered easily.
2 Start each new section on a new sheet of paper (for the same reason).
3 Leave a wide margin so that you can add notes and make amendments.

The format   Your finished assignment should be presented in an organized way. It is helpful to know at the start how it will finally be composed. Below is an actual example of the list of contents of an assignment.

<u>List of Contents</u>

		Pages
1.	Introduction	1 – 4
2.	Investigation	5 – 9
3.	Analysis	10 – 12
4.	Methods	13 – 16
5.	Conclusion	17
6.	Bibliography	18
7.	Appendices	19 – 52

This example shows a standard format which can be used if you have a completely free choice of what to do and/or your teacher does not give you any specific guidance. This format will help you to demonstrate your achievement of the assessment objectives. For instance, in the 'Methods' section you will consider how you approached the assignment. Hopefully you will see and comment on the merits and weaknesses of your method. This indicates a high level of performance in the skill of evaluation (refer back to table 1.1).

What goes in each section?

1 Introduction

This section explains the purpose of the assignment and outlines the problem you are considering. In this part you should relate your chosen assignment to your syllabus. You need to read through your notes and skim through your textbook to see which topics in your course can be applied. The more links which you can establish between your subject and

Stress the 'Economics' aspect of your assignment.

the different aspects of the course, the more marks you will receive for information and application. You can also bring in general **economic concepts** which are relevant to your problem. This idea is explored in more detail in Section Seven.

2 Investigation

Here you should describe your research. You should explain how you collected your information and present the data which you have acquired (see Sections Five and Six).

3 Analysis

In this section you should consider the **meaning** of your data. You need to consider, and provide answers to, questions such as:

(a) What does the data show?

(b) Is it accurate?

(c) Is it biased?

(d) Does it help to answer the question under consideration?

Guidance on such analysis is given in Section Seven.

4 Methods

In this section you should discuss in detail how you went about the assignment: **what** you did, **when** and, most importantly, **why** you chose to do what you did.

Don't be afraid of criticizing your work or highlighting the faults. This is also where you should describe any **problems** which arose and **mistakes** you made. Say how you dealt with them and suggest **ways in which the work could be improved** if it were tried again in the future.

5 Conclusion

Your title should be in the form of a question or an hypothesis (see Section Four). In this section you must give an **answer** to the question or a **verdict** on the hypothesis. It must be supported by **reasons**. It may be a **qualified** answer, recognizing the **limitations** of your research.

6 Bibliography

This is simply a list of books, newspapers and articles which you have consulted in your research. Each time you use a publication you should note down the author, the title and publication details (publisher, date) on a piece of file paper. This list will be the basis of your final bibliography. The presentation of the bibliography is explained in Section Eight.

7 Appendices

An appendix is material which is 'added on' to explain or illustrate your main text. You should include here **examples of raw materials** used. For instance, if you have conducted a sample, a completed **survey sheet** should be put in this section. If you have written **letters** to various 'experts', their **replies** should be included along with copies of any **newspaper or magazine articles** you have referred to. Appendices are considered further in Section Eight.

When do I write each section?

Present your work neatly and clearly.

This is the order in which you are advised to prepare the final versions of the sections:

List of contents	9
Introduction	2
Investigation	3
Analysis	5
Methods	6
Conclusion	7
Bibliography	1–4
Appendix	8

Notice that the order of writing the sections is different from the order in which they are finally compiled. For instance, you should build up the bibliography as you go along, although it comes toward the end of the finished assignment and the list of contents is the last thing to be completed, although it will be placed at the beginning of the finished work.

✔ Checklist

DO
- plan ahead
- consult your diary regularly
- try to keep to your schedule
- write on file paper
- use a separate file for each assignment and subject
- use the standard format (unless your teacher has specified another)
- start each section on a separate sheet
- be prepared to re-write

DON'T
- leave your assignment until the last minute
- panic if you get behind schedule (you should have built in some 'leeway')
- expect perfection at first (or at last!)
- tear up first drafts (attempts) – you may wish to refer to them later

Titles

You will not always be given a free choice of topic or assignment title. Some examination groups set specific titles and sometimes your teacher may decide that all the class will pursue the same general theme.

Popular themes

The most common themes suggested (and in some cases actually specified) by the examination groups are:

(a) A case study of a firm

(b) A study of a local issue

(c) A study of a national/international problem

(d) An exercise in personal economic decision-making

(e) A study of an area

1 A case study of a firm

For Economics, a case study of a firm, shop, or enterprise should look at the economic decision-making of the business. As obtaining information will probably be your biggest problem you need a contact in the organization. If you have a part-time job, it would be a good idea to choose the organization which employs you. If not, you might choose the employer of a parent or a relative. You must arrange a visit, in order to gather information for your case study.

If the organization is small, e.g. a corner shop, you could cover many aspects of the business. However, with a large enterprise you cannot hope to do that. You will need to select a specific area to study.

Example

The East Midlands Gas Board District Office based in Grimsby has three main functions: engineering, marketing and administration. A case study of up to 1000 words would be best devoted to just one of the three functions, by looking at just one department.

This type of assignment is mainly descriptive and involves collecting information from various sources. The identification of relevant material and proper organization and presentation of that material will be central to a successful assignment.

2 A study of a local issue

This issue could be:

(a) a business problem, e.g. the effect of the closure of a factory.

(b) an economic issue, e.g. the arguments for and against the building of a new supermarket/hotel/car park.

(c) a social problem, e.g. the pollution of a local estuary by a chemical factory.

This sort of assignment will require the collection of opinions and may involve you in conducting a survey and interviewing interested parties. Your local newspaper will be a vital source of information and opinions. You will be expected to make reasoned judgments.

3 A study of a national/international issue

More general topics are covered in this sort of assignment, e.g. regional policy in the U.K. The approach involves little or no fieldwork. The accent will be on information gathering, the selection of main factors which bear on the problem and critical discussion of the key points.

4 An exercise in personal economic decision-making

A very specific problem is considered in this type of assignment. For example, when buying an expensive item is it better to save up before buying, or buy on credit? In this example, you could research the interest rates charged by different forms of credit (e.g. hire purchase, credit cards, bank loans). The assignment will be heavily focused on the understanding and presentation of the various options available.

5 A study of an area

The area involved could be small, e.g. a local shopping centre, a village or an industrial estate, or relatively large, e.g. your county. You could classify the business functions and types in a small area and explain the importance of each to the community. Another popular topic is the local market for a particular product, looking at either the supply and demand aspects, or the way in which various services (e.g. advertising) are employed.

You will usually need to carry out a survey because of the lack of published information relating to your specific area. Maps will be an important method of presenting your information.

Ideas Questions and hypotheses

Your coursework assignment should deal with a **problem** which involves Economics. It is worthwhile phrasing the problem as a **question**. You can then offer possible answers which can be critically evaluated demonstrating your analytical skills.

Example

Problem: New car.
Question: Where are new cars advertised?
Possible answer: New cars are advertised mostly in daily newspapers.

Some economics assignments are examples of a process known as **hypothesis testing**. The above problem – question – possible answer approach is at the basis of the process. The proposed answer becomes an **hypothesis** which can be used as a title. Your task would be to test this hypothesis by collecting data, interpreting it and applying it to the original problem. You would then be expected to judge whether or not the information which you have obtained proves or disproves your hypothesis.

Your title could be a **question** to which you try to discover an answer. The sorts of questions used usually begin:
Why does . . . ?
How do . . . ?
To what extent is . . . ?
Where is . . . ?

Examples

Why does the standard of living in Britain vary so much between the North West and the South East?

How do local firms in the building trade compete?

To what extent is the proposed 'community charge' unfair?

Where should the new supermarket be sited?

Have you any ideas?

You need to think of an issue or problem which interests you. It must be something which can be related to Economics. It could be linked to a **part-time job** or to a **hobby**. It is also ideal to choose an idea or theme for which you have ready access to information.

Examples

Part-time jobs	Possible questions
Shop assistant	Is the shop efficiently run?
Shelf filler	How does the shop attract customers?
Delivery boy/girl	Why was the shop located where it is?
	What competition is there in retailing?
	How do our credit facilities compare with other retailers?
Mail-order agent	To what extent is mail-order successful?
Football coupon collector	How could the organization of my round be
Newspaper boy/girl	improved?
Waiter/waitress	How/why are part-time staff used?
Amusement arcade cashier	To what extent are service and leisure industries replacing manufacturing in this area of Britain?
Baby-sitting	What factors determine the amount paid to baby-sitters?

Hobbies	Possible questions
Sports	Is *your sport* efficiently advertised?
Pastimes	Why have the prices of *equipment/entrance fees* risen/fallen in recent years?
	What economic factors explain the increase in participation in leisure activities?

How ideas become titles

1 Give your problem an economics dimension

It is a good idea to include an economics concept in the title. Refer to your notes, your textbook and the subject content of your syllabus for ideas. Suitable concepts include:

price	resources	sales
market	choice	income
demand	scarcity	competition
efficiency	location	private sector
costs/benefits	production	local economy

Concepts used in your title will need to be explained in the assignment, enabling you to demonstrate your **'knowledge and understanding'** skills (outlined in the assessment objectives). You will also have to **apply** the concepts to the particular problem.

2 Choose a narrowly-defined topic

If you select a wide area, you risk getting buried in mountains of information. For instance, the hypothesis 'Advertising is wasteful' would be too general. It would be better to look at the advertising of a particular product e.g. advertising of deodorants. With questions arising from local issues (e.g. siting a new supermarket) the emphasis will be fairly well-defined.

3 Choose a specific aspect of the narrow topic

For example, having decided to prepare a case study of the local steel mill (you have access to information because your father is a line manager there), you should choose a specific economic aspect of the organization: e.g. 'The factors determining the location of the Abbey steel works in Port Talbot', not 'The British steel industry' or 'The Margam Abbey Works'.

4 Use value-laden words (or phrases)

If you use such words in your title or hypothesis you will be lead into **evaluation and judgment**.

Examples

Is A the best/worse solution to . . . ?
Would B be good/bad for . . . ?
Is C a suitable/unsuitable policy to . . . ?
Will D be successful/unsuccessful in . . . ?

Provocative adverbs can also be used in your question or hypothesis. Such adverbs cause controversy.

Examples

Supermarket prices are always cheaper than corner shops.
Why have house prices risen a lot recently?
Only public sector wage increases can be controlled by the Government.

5 Comparisons

Comparisons also force you to make judgments. You could either state an hypothesis that 'A is better/worse than B for . . .' or ask the question 'Is A better/worse than B for . . .?'.

Examples

The wasteland in . . . would be better developed as a playground than as an amusement arcade.
Local government should be financed locally rather than centrally.

✔ Checklist

DO • choose a subject you are interested in
  • choose a subject on which you can get information
  • deal with a problem
  • make your title a question or an hypothesis
  • use economic ideas

DON'T • make your topic too broad
  • avoid controversy
  • forget the Economics angle

Collection of data

There is more to the collection of data than just finding out the views of different people. Therefore this section is divided up into several subsections, each dealing with important aspects of information gathering.

Background

There are several general things which you need to bear in mind before you start the actual investigation:

The need for a diary

You should keep a diary of your activities from the outset. This is necessary not only for planning but also for the final written report. In the section of your report entitled 'Investigation' you will outline **how** you went about the assignment. The way in which you have operated will be as important for assessment as the tentative conclusions you reach. Keeping a record of your work should include:

– **when** you collected the data, i.e. the dates and times
– **where** you collected the data, i.e. the locations and visits made
– **why** you collected the data in a certain way, e.g. 'It was easy and quick to produce questionnaires for my dad to distribute at work.'

Example

DATE	ACTIVITY	VENUE	REASON(S)
Oct 10	Distributed 10 sheets	school	easy, part sample
12	Got 8 back	school	2 forgot
13	Gave Dad 10 sheets	home	for work mates
	Gave Mum 10 sheets	home	for people in her office
17	Got 1 school sheet back	school	Sugden forgot again
	Gave out 2 more	school	extras – just in case

Safety

Your own personal safety is very important. If you visit a factory or shop then the proprietors will probably make you aware of the hazards. However, if you are conducting a survey on the street there are certain precautions you should take:

- Make sure someone knows where you will be and when you expect to be back home (or back in school).
- Always carry some identification and a phonecard or coins for a public telephone.
- Be aware of traffic and crowds – remember the basic road safety rules.
- Try not to visit lonely places where you may be at risk.
- Conduct surveys during daylight, rather than after dark.
- If possible, work with someone else, or make sure a friend is nearby, so that help is at hand if anything untoward happens.

Headteacher
Mrs. V. Tolhurst
B.Sc.

Tel. (0472) 694888

MATTHEW HUMBERSTONE SCHOOL
CHATSWORTH PLACE
CLEETHORPES
DN35 9NF

To whom it may concern

G.C.S.E. Economics Course Work Assignment, 1989-90

The bearer of this letter is a Fifth Year student at Matthew Humberstone School involved in researching and writing a Course Work Assignment for the new G.C.S.E. Economics examinations.

The Assignment concerns advertising and it will be necessary for the student to ask members of the public and business people some questions about the products they buy and sell.

I hope you will be prepared to help by giving the student a few minutes of your time.

Thank you very much.

Yours sincerely,

Valerie Tolhurst

Mrs. V. Tolhurst,
Headteacher.

Fig. 5.1 A standard Letter of Authority

Courtesy

When undertaking research good manners need to be shown at all times. Courtesy is particularly important when you wish to visit people to seek information. **Write in advance** to your would-be interviewees, briefly explaining why you wish to interview them. When (if) you receive a favourable reply, either write or telephone to fix a date and time for an interview. You could also enquire if the 'expert' minds being tape-recorded and send a copy of the questions you will ask. If people are lukewarm about helping you, don't pester them.

On the day of the interview make an effort to dress smartly, as well as taking the necessary documents and writing equipment. Make sure that you know exactly where you are going. Try to arrive at least 10 minutes early – some organizations are very large and it may take time to find the room you want. Be suitably thankful at the end of the interview.

In general, you will need **permission** to be on private property (e.g. a factory) or outside someone's premises (e.g. a shop). Your teacher/school should have a **standard letter** similar to the one shown in Figure 5.1, which you can send to the shopkeeper/factory manager beforehand, or show as necessary to shopkeepers, customers, traffic wardens, etc.

You may also need written permission to be late home from school.

Types of data

In research, a distinction is usually made between **primary and secondary sources of information**. 'Primary' material refers to information collected by you specifically for your assignment, whilst 'secondary' information has been acquired by other people. However, secondary sources are also available for your use. In Economics both types of information are very useful.

The main sources of data to be considered are classified below:

Primary	**Secondary**
Questionnaires/surveys	Books
Direct observation	Newspapers and magazines
Experiments	Official statistics
Letters	

Each of these sources are discussed in detail a little later in this chapter.

Choice of data collection method

If possible, a variety of techniques should be used to collect data. This will impress the examiners and score marks. However, this strategy will only work if each method used is **appropriate** and **properly applied**.

Your choice may be limited by:

1 The setting for the research – if the assignment is teacher-led and closely controlled then you will probably have to operate as your teacher requests.

2 The time available – if you have eight months to complete your assignment you will have far more opportunity for field work carried out in stages, than if you have a four-week deadline.

3 The willingness of other people to cooperate – if you want to investigate a local dispute and the participants are not willing to be interviewed, you will need to use a different method (or choose a different topic!).

4 Your own personality – for example, if you are quiet and shy then you might not want to interview strangers in the street.

5 Finance – although most resources will be provided in school, some techniques, such as those involving visits, correspondence and experiments, may require your own personal expenditure (or your parents'), so consider costs before you embark on an 'unusual' assignment.

Disaster strikes!

The disaster probably won't be as dramatic as the one in the cartoon, but your original plans may not work out for some reason. This often happens. For instance, several people you were hoping to interview might let you down. Such problems should be recorded in your diary and referred to when you write up the investigation and discuss your methods. You will need to choose an alternative approach and learn that things do not always run smoothly and/or as you want them to.

Don't panic! If you followed the advice given earlier, you will have some 'slack' in your timetable to cope with such problems.

Teachers

Your teacher is probably your most important resource. He/she can direct you to useful sources of information and may even make assignments from previous years available for guidance. This is particularly true when your assignment is about a local issue.

However, there are probably 20 other students in your class who also need his/her help. If class time is not made available for you to consult your teacher, you should make your own arrangements. The end of a lesson or briefly after school might be appropriate times. Most teachers will be willing to help and will probably be flattered by your request.

You should make out a **list** of what you wish to ask in order to save the valuable time of your hard-pressed teacher. Prepare two copies of your list so that you can give one to your teacher to remind him/her of your questions, if he/she does not have time to deal with them immediately. (You should, of course, keep the other copy.) Your teacher will be marking your assignment but this does not mean he/she cannot help you. The examining groups do require that you acknowledge any such help though. Your teacher will have a form for you to complete and include with your assignment.

Investigation techniques – Primary data

Surveys

The main method of primary data collection which you are likely to use is a survey, based on a questionnaire. This method can be divided into four stages:

1 Sampling
2 Stratification
3 The questionnaire
4 Conducting the survey

1 The sample

You will need a sample of people to answer your survey. A sample is a selection of people from the population which you are studying. You have to take a sample because you will not have the time or the money necessary to question everyone who might be appropriate.

Samples are supposed to be **representative**, i.e. the people interviewed should, on average, have the same characteristics as the population in which you are interested. For instance, if you are conducting a fashion survey on women's clothes and you know from your background reading that 10 per cent of women's clothes are bought by men (as presents, etc), then 10 per cent of your sample should be men.

Unrepresentative samples give results from which generalizations cannot be made. Unfortunately, with limited time and resources, you will not be able to contact enough people to give you a truly representative sample. Opinion poll surveys with 1000 or more respondents have a 3 per cent sampling error. By using as many as 100 people your results would still not be representative enough to draw definite conclusions.

It is best to have **about 30 respondents** in your sample. If you have many more you will have too much data to process, many less (less than 20) and your conclusions will be very speculative indeed.

It does not matter that your sample is small and unrepresentative as long as you:

– clearly state that it is

– explain why

– treat your results with caution

Such comments should be included in the 'Methods' and 'Conclusion' sections of your assignment.

2 Stratification – Quota sampling

Despite the general limitations which have just been explained, you can do a lot with your sample of 30 if you **stratify** (or segment) it. This means that you divide your sample into people of different types, e.g. male and female – this would be stratifying (segmenting) by **sex**. Similarly, a sample can be stratified by **age groups**, e.g. 'under 18', '18 to 65', and 'over 65'. Age groupings used will vary between surveys depending on the topic. For instance, the age groups mentioned above would not be suitable if you were surveying the part-time jobs of schoolchildren. If you stratify by age, choose the age boundaries carefully and give reasons for your choice in the 'Methods' section of your assignment. Samples are sometimes stratified according to the areas where people live and/or social class but such divisions are not recommended.

You must interview a **specified quota** (number) of people from each group. This keeps the sample 'balanced' and allows comparisons to be made between groups in the analysis. When choosing the size of your sample and how you will stratify it, bear in mind the time available and how easy, or difficult it will be to contact people in each of your groups.

Example

In the following example, the sample is stratified by sex and age. Out of the 30 people, there are 15 men and 15 women. There are also 10 people under 18 years of age, 10 between 18 and 65, and 10 over 65.

Fig. 5.2 A stratification grid

	SEX		
AGE	Male	Female	Total
U18	5	5	10
18–65	5	5	10
65+	5	5	10
Total	15	15	30

A grid like the one on the previous page (Figure 5.2) is very useful. Notice that you have acquired 12 different groups in total. Each box in the grid contains a group with certain definitive characteristics. For instance, the top left-hand box contains 5 males under 18. That group's survey answers could be contrasted with those of the 5 females over the age of 65 (bottom right-hand box).

It is worth noting the **advantages and drawbacks** of quota sampling. You should refer to them in your report. The main advantages are that it is **simple, quick and cheap**. Unfortunately, it is **unlikely to be accurate** because each group will be quite small and it depends on your selection of the people in each group. For instance, if your quota calls for 10 people of working age and you ask one of your parents to distribute your questionnaire, they will probably give them to friends doing similar work rather than to a wide range of working people, so your sample will not be very representative of the whole population of working people.

3 Questionnaires

A questionnaire is the **list of questions** used to collect information. It may be used either in a **survey** or in an **interview**.

The questionnaire needs a brief **title** relating to your research. You must reassure your respondents that their answers will be kept **confidential**. **Information on the respondents** is also required for the later analysis. This will be related to your stratification. You will probably be interested in their **age**, **sex** and/or **occupation** and you should include a section to gather this information. After the specific questions related to your assignment title, '**thank you**' will provide a suitable ending.

Questions

The questions can be of two types:
1 Open-ended questions: These give **no guidance** to the person answering, e.g. 'What factors would influence your choice of car?' These questions are easy to devise but you may not get the kind of answers which you seek and it may be **difficult to classify the answers** which you do get (see 'Coding' in Section Seven).

2 Closed questions: These questions give the respondent guidance. Often a set of possible answers is given and the respondent is asked to choose one by performing a specific task which is usually fairly simple. For example, in the sample survey shown in Figure 5.3, the respondent has to tick the relevant boxes.

Closed questions are most useful when **opinions** are sought. You can make a statement, then ask people to tick a box indicating their feelings on the subject.

Example

'Unemployment benefit is too high.' Please tick whichever of the following statements fits your view on this matter:

strongly agree ☐

agree ☐

don't know/not sure ☐

disagree ☐

strongly disagree ☐

Coding and analysis of answers are easier with closed questions because your several **possible replies are predetermined** (known in advance). However, they may **over-simplify** a problem by limiting the possible

A SURVEY ON CLOTHES PURCHASING

PLEASE TICK APPROPRIATE BOXES.

SEX: male ☐   AGE: 10 – 20 ☐   40 – 60 ☐
female ☐   20 – 40 ☐   60 + ☐

(1) WHERE DO YOU BUY MOST OF YOUR CLOTHES:
 (i) Dress / Clothes Shops ☐   (ii) Supermarkets ☐
 (iii) Mail- Order Catalogues ☐   (iv) Department Stores ☐
 (v) Market Stalls ☐   (vi) Tailors ☐
 (vii) OTHER (Please list): _____

(2) FACTORS WHICH INFLUENCE YOU MOST IN YOUR CHOICE
 OF CLOTHES (TICK UP TO THREE BOXES):
 (i) Fashion ☐   (ii) Colour ☐   (iii) Price ☐
 (iv) Quality ☐   (v) Sex Appeal ☐
 (vi) OTHER (Please list): _____

(3) IF YOU BUY/BOUGHT YOUR CLOTHES FROM A SHOP WOULD
 YOU BUY FROM:
 (i) A large national company who sell a number of products,
   e.g. Binns, Tescos ?   ☐
 (ii) A national company who specialize in clothes,
   e.g. Dorothy Perkins, Burtons?   ☐
 (iii) A local shop, e.g. Raffles ?   ☐

(4) DO ADVERTS INFLUENCE YOUR CHOICE OF CLOTHES ?
 (i) Yes   ☐
 (ii) No   ☐
 (iii) Sometimes   ☐

(5) IN GENERAL, DO YOU PAY MUCH ATTENTION TO ADVERTS?
 (i) Yes   ☐
 (ii) No   ☐
 (iii) Sometimes   ☐

Thank You

Fig. 5.3 A questionnaire of closed questions

replies and the respondents may be influenced by the alternatives offered. The **order** in which the alternatives are presented may also affect the answer given. You could point out such possible deficiencies in your 'Conclusion' if you have used closed questions.

The questions asked should be:

- **short** – Long rambling questions may cause confusion. Generally, questions should be less than 13 words to be easily understood.

- **clear** – Avoid ambiguous words. For example, the question 'How much attention do you pay to adverts?' has at least two meanings. 'How much attention' could refer either to depth of concentration or the amount of time spend watching adverts.

- **specific** – Only question one idea, or piece of information, at a time. Avoid using 'and' in survey questions.

- **unbiased** – Avoid words such as 'good' and 'bad' which might lead respondents to a certain viewpoint. That is, unless you are then seeking people's opinions/reactions to a statement.

- **few** – If your survey has less than five questions it will probably seem inconsequential, but respondents may get bored with more than eight questions. Too many questions can also lead to lots of data which can be difficult to process.

The example opposite, Figure 5.4, which combines both open and closed questions, illustrates much of the advice given above.

You should always prepare a **rough draft** of the questions. It is a good idea to **try them out** on family or friends (and to ask your teacher to have a look at them if he/she has time).

When you are satisfied that they work (i.e. that they will give you the information you need) write (or type) the questionnaire very neatly and have it duplicated (or photocopied) in a sufficient quantity. You will need enough for your sample, a copy for your appendix section and be sure to have some spares.

4 Conducting the survey

There are two basic approaches to fieldwork:

(a) Distributing questionnaires

You give people the questionnaire to complete at their leisure and ask them to return it to you at a future date. This approach requires you to prepare and duplicate your questionnaire. Your teacher should be able to give you the necessary materials or provide access to photocopying.

The advantages of this method are that it **saves time** and avoids the possible embarrassment in asking questions face to face. However, you cannot definitely know if the person to whom you gave the sheet does actually complete it with their own knowledge and/or views. In addition, **you are not available to explain** any possible difficulties in the questions (but these should be few if you have tried out your questions before preparing the good copy of your questionnaire). For this and other reasons, some of the sheets may not be returned promptly or at all. These problems may slow down your research.

Despite the potential difficulties, my students tend to prefer distributing survey sheets, mainly because it is a lot quicker than interviewing.

(b) Interviews

You ask the people in your sample the questions which you have prepared and write down their answers.

The advantage of this is that **you are there to clarify any uncertainties** that arise. However, interviews are **time-consuming** and you or your interviewees may be embarrassed by the situation or even by the questions.

<u>SURVEY</u>

<u>REGIONAL PREFERENCE</u>

1. AGE   UNDER 18   19-40   41-65   65+

     [✓]   [ ]   [ ]   [ ]

2. SEX   MALE   FEMALE

     [✓]   [ ]

3. EMPLOYED   YES   NO   STUDENT

     [ ]   [ ]   [✓]

4. DO YOU OWN A   DISHWASHER   DEEP FREEZE

     Yes   No   Yes   No

     [✓]   [ ]   [✓]   [ ]

     TELEPHONE   MOTOR CAR

     Yes   No   Yes   No

     [✓]   [ ]   [✓]   [ ]

5. DO YOU LIKE LIVING IN HUMBERSIDE   V.Much   It's ok   Not much   No

     [ ]   [✓]   [ ]   [ ]

6. WOULD YOU PREFER LIVING ELSEWHERE IN U.K.   Yes   No

     [ ]   [✗]

(a) IF SO, WHERE?   [—————]

(b) IF NOT, WHY DO YOU LIKE IT HERE

     [LOTS TO DO]

7. WOULD YOU LIKE TO LIVE IN THE SOUTH EAST   Yes   No

     [ ]   [✗]

(a) IF NOT WHY   [TOO CROWDED, EXPENSIVE]

(b) IF SO, WHY   [—————]

Fig. 5.4 A questionnaire with open and closed questions

If possible, interviews should be tape-recorded, so that you can replay them and analyse them later.

If you are going out to directly interview adults make sure that you have a **letter of authority** from your school. An example of such a letter was given in Figure 5.1.

Have your **blank grid** of the stratified sample with you so that you can mark in each box the type of person interviewed. If the quota for a particular group is five, once you have interviewed five of that type you can concentrate on filling your other quotas. You may fail to fill a box, i.e. you may not reach the full quota for a particular group. This is a common problem in most research and has to to be accepted. Report the problem in your 'investigations' section and take it into consideration when drawing conclusions from your results.

If you use a survey, you should briefly explain why you chose the approach you used in the 'Methods' section of your assignment.

✓ Checklist – Surveys

DO
- prepare a rough draft and 'try out' your questions
- give your questionnaire a title
- ask short, clear and specific questions
- stratify your sample and use a grid
- obtain details on age, sex, etc
- take a letter of authority
- remember the safety rules

DON'T
- ask biased or ambiguous questions
- ask too many questions
- forget a 'thank you'
- pester people
- run short of questionnaires

Interviewing 'experts'

As well as, or instead of, interviews related to a short questionnaire, interviews may be conducted with other adults, specialists and/or people with particular knowledge of the issue/topic you are looking at. Your interviews with such people will be longer and more detailed than the questionnaire interviews just described.

When you are after opinions, as in survey research, virtually anyone can be approached. However, when you are seeking **facts**, you need to consult 'experts', or people directly involved with an issue. For instance, if you are studying possible motorway by-pass routes in your area, you should contact the district's Chief Planning Officer, or an official in his department. You could also interview the leader of a local pressure group and affected residents.

A general problem of this investigation technique is that your 'expert' may give **biased** answers. So if you are dealing with an issue, you need to get a variety of opinions to enable you to reach a balanced judgment.

Example

A student took as his title: 'Does Romford need another supermarket?'

As well as conducting survey research amongst unemployed people and residents near the proposed site, he sought a range of 'expert' opinions from:
– a representative of the new supermarket company;
– spokespeople from the existing foodstores in the area;
– the manager of the local job centre.

Before conducting your interview, prepare a list of important questions to which you want answers. (As suggested earlier, you might send a copy of this list to the 'expert' before the interview, especially if you will be asking for detailed information.) It is advisable to have some **follow-up questions** which you can use if you think that answers to the initial questions are vague and/or evasive. When the list is written out, leave spaces (several lines per question) to write the answers. In the example related to assessing the need for Romford's new supermarket, the student's questions included:

Example

Will it create more jobs?
Follow-up: What sort of jobs will they be?
Will existing jobs go?
Will it cause traffic congestion?
Follow-up: Will it reduce traffic congestion elsewhere?
Do the people want another supermarket?
Follow-up: Why do some people want it?

Practice the interview. You could read your questions out to a friend or parent. This makes you familiar with the questions. It will give you confidence and help the actual interview run more smoothly.

During the interview, try to stick to the questions and note the answers given. After the interview, read through the answers which you have noted and add things you remember but didn't manage to write down at the time. You should do this very soon afterwards while the interview is fresh in your mind. If you have been able to tape record the interview, this will enable yo to 'go over' any points you were not sure about at your leisure, rather than rely on your memory which (like mine) is probably fallible!

Some of the answers may be irrelevant – do not be afraid to reject the unusable parts of the interview. You will probably be able to quote some of the best material when you write up your 'investigation'. In the 'Methods' section you should mention who you contacted and why you chose them. Also describe any problems which arose (e.g. tape recorder jammed) and suggest ways in which future similar research could be improved.

✓ Checklist – Interviews

- Make an appointment.
- Send a copy of your questions to the interviewee.
- Ask if you can tape-record the interview.
- Have some follow-up questions.
- Dress smartly and arrive early.
- Review your notes as soon as possible after the interview.
- Write a thank you letter.

Observation

This approach involves watching and recording people's behaviour. For instance, if you were conducting a shopping survey you might **count** how many people entered a particular shop and **time** how long they took to buy the goods. You need to be **unobtrusive** because you are interested in their normal behaviour, rather than how they would react if they knew that they were being watched.

It might be appropriate to take **photographs** to show a particular scene at a certain time, e.g. during a traffic survey. Generally though you need only note down the events which occur.

Have sheets of file paper or specially prepared sheets on which to note observations, a pen which works (and a spare pen!). The recording sheets should have the basic information, i.e. the place and time, at the top, as well as the specific information which you are seeking and spaces to record your observations.

Example

A shopping survey was carried out by a group of three students. One counted people entering a shop, the second counted people who stopped and looked in at the window, the third, those who passed by. A copy of their specially prepared recording sheet is shown below.

SHOPPING SURVEY

DAY _____   PLACE _____

Time started _____   TIME finished _____ TOTAL TIME____

PEOPLE ENTERING SHOP   TOTAL

MEN   _____

WOMEN   _____

CHILDREN _____

COUPLES _____

FAMILIES _____   GRAND TOTAL

PEOPLE LOOKING IN WINDOW   TOTAL

MEN   _____

WOMEN   _____

CHILDREN _____

COUPLES _____

FAMILIES _____

                                         GRAND TOTAL

PEOPLE PASSING BY   TOTAL

MEN   _____

WOMEN   _____

CHILDREN _____

COUPLES _____

FAMILIES _____

                                         GRAND TOTAL

As a research method, observation is often a useful **starting point** because it could give you some ideas to be researched further. But there are pitfalls. For example, when watching potential buyers and clocking their time in a shop, you may be *distracted* and so miss someone leaving. If you want to collect accurate statistics, this method is probably inferior to the interview and the survey.

Experiments

These are generally to be avoided. Sociologists argue that people behave unnaturally when they know that they are involved in an experiment. This suggests that any results which are obtained may be unreliable. An experiment must produce tangible results which can be evaluated. To achieve this you must have a clear idea of the aim of your experiment before you start and you must keep it simple. A large amount of cooperation is often needed which you may not be able to organize in the limited time available for an assignment.

Mini-business enterprises can provide scope for successful assignments, e.g. running a coffee bar or operating a car-wash scheme. You could use the mini-business to investigate or demonstrate some economic concepts, e.g. costs and revenue, price demand and supply, elasticity of demand, competition, etc. Experiments reveal the effects of actions, so lend themselves to analysis and evaluation, skills on which your assignment will be assessed.

The **design** or **planning** stage of an experiment is vitally important. The conditions under which the experiment will be undertaken need to be decided in advance. They will probably require your **teacher's permission** and possibly the help of friends. It is a good idea to have a **dummy run** to check that everything works and, if not, to iron out any faults. (This should be reported in your 'Methods' section.) You may wish to vary certain aspects of the experiment at different times. The next example illustrates how this might be done using different production runs.

You will probably need **specialist equipment**, e.g. the coffee bar idea requires basic coffee-making facilities. You will have to arrange **storage** and ensure the **safety** of the equipment. Any **helpers** will need to be thoroughly briefed on their roles and responsibilities. On each occasion the experiment is undertaken **accurate recording** of the results is essential. This could be done by taking notes (direct observation), tape- or video-recording. (Audio or video cassettes can be included in your final assignment presentation.)

Even if the results obtained are unfavourable or inconsistent, stick with them and try to explain them in your 'Methods', 'Analysis' and 'Conclusions' sections.

Example

The following example is an experiment which took place entirely in the classroom. The example has been taken from a Chief Moderator's report (NEA Economics A, 1988).

> 'One centre investigated specialization and the division of labour by converting the classroom into a sandwich bar. In the course of the enquiry students explored a range of ideas, concepts, and terms – including alternative costs of production, revenues, production processes, comparative advantage and many more.
>
> A short extract from one of the pupil's accounts of the structure of the activity is given below:
>
> > "Our experiment was to determine what were the advantages and disadvantages of specialization and division of labour by means of a classroom production exercise. We set out to examine and explore differences in attitudes, quality of product, capital expenditure required, speed, efficiency and several other factors.
> >
> > *List of ingredients needed*
> >
> > *Prices and total*
> >
> > | | |
> > |---|---|
> > | 24 white baps | 1.37 |
> > | 6 tomatoes | 0.46 |
> > | 1lb 14oz cheese | 1.76 |
> > | salad cream | 0.34 |
> > | St Ivel Gold | 0.70 |
> > | sandwich bags | 0.35 |
> > | TOTAL | £4.98 |
> >
> > 2 pence for carrier bag making a total of £5.50

<u>Production run 1</u>

On the first production run there were six people working, two people counting the amount of tools used and one person with a stop watch. There were some tools which were placed in the middle of the table, six knives, six plates, the grater, one sharp knife, one fork and two spoons.

The ingredients were placed in the middle of the table. When everybody was ready, the timer was started and everybody just delved in, making two baps each, one was butter with cheese and tomato, the other was salad cream and cheese also buttered. The workers made the baps as neat and efficient as was possible, wrapping them at the end. They were timed from start to finish.

People were being paid £2.40 (which we had found out was the going local rate in a sandwich bar) an hour which was really being wasted as some people were doing nothing."

On the second run, division of labour was employed and the students reflected on the quantity of capital required. The students then calculated labour costs, capital costs and material costs using the two systems and added a notional 10 per cent for profits under each system. They were able to make calculations based on average costs and prices.

Each student involved with the above piece of coursework produced three coursework assignments for assessment. All students were able to show what they knew, understood and could do. There was a good spread of marks and all students showed that they had benefited from their course by being given the opportunity actively to engage in economic enquiry.'

✔ Checklist – Experiments

DO • get any necessary permission
• check the feasibility of the experiment (time, expense, etc)
• obtain the necessary equipment
• have a dummy run
• keep accurate records

DON'T • be over-ambitious
• forget to brief any helpers thoroughly
• leave equipment and supplies lying about
• fiddle the figures
• be frightened to report a failure

Letters

Correspondence can be an effective way of **obtaining information**. For this purpose, the approach may be specific or **general**. For instance, you might write to several companies seeking company annual reports in order to acquire general background knowledge about an industry.

If you are seeking **specific information** you should write to an 'expert' or specialist within an organization. For example, when seeking guidance from a Gas Board about the viability of providing gas to a small village, you should write to the 'Public Relations Officer' of the local board.

You might also send letters to seek **opinions**. If you intend to contact a number of people in this way then a survey sheet with a **standard covering letter** will save a lot of time. However, if you only need the views of a few, probably local, experts, then individually written letters will be more personal and effective.

Get your letters checked for spelling, grammar, punctuation.

Initially, compose a **draft letter**. Get your teacher, or a parent, to check it and comment on it. After making any changes, write (or type) it neatly. Do not forget to **sign it legibly**. Always **keep a copy** in your assignment file. Make a separate section for correspondence, including a copy of each letter and a note of when they were sent and the replies received.

If you do not get a reply within two weeks, then try a **'phone call**. If this has no effect then, in the interests of time, you should abandon the contact and try someone else. You can report such 'failures' in your 'Methods' and 'Investigations' sections.

Copies of your letters and replies should be put in the 'Appendix' section of your finished assignment.

The following example is a standard letter which could be sent to several local organizations. You could get their addresses out of *Yellow Pages*. It is usually a good idea to address the letter to a relevant person or a specific department. For example, if your assignment concerns advertising it should be addressed to Sales (or Marketing) Director.

Example

Your telephone number

Your address

Their address

Date

Dear Sir/Madam,
  I am currently studying G.C.S.E Economics at _____
One of my assignments is to investigate _____
and I would be grateful if you could help me.
  As your firm is involved in _____, I wondered if you could provide me with some information. I would also like to visit your _____ if possible.

  Yours faithfully

Schoolname

Brief summary of your topic

Your topic

Firm/shop/factory/etc

Your signature

Your name printed very neatly

If the organization is helpful, write again requesting more **specific information**. Be a bit pushy! However, do not forget that as a matter of etiquette further letters should begin with the recipient's name ('Dear Mr/Ms/ . . .') and end 'Yours sincerely, . . .'.

DO ● prepare a draft
　　● write to a particular person within an organization or company
　　● sign your name legibly
　　● keep a copy of actual letters sent

DON'T ● be too pushy at first
　　● send out a questionnaire without a covering letter
　　● wait forever for replies

Secondary data

Secondary data is collected by looking at **existing information**, reading and making notes from different sources. Sometimes such work is referred to as '**desktop research**' (because it can be done at a desk!).

The following sections look at the most commonly used sources of secondary data:

Your notebook

This is probably your most accessible written source of information. In it, you will have summarized the main points of the topics studied in your Economics classes.

Once you have chosen your title, or been given the theme, you should consider which **Economics topics** could be relevant to your chosen assignment. Then read your notes on these topics to refresh your memory on the main ideas. As you read, **make notes** of the main points on file paper.

Example

In the following example, an assignment on 'the North–South divide' used ideas from eight topics:

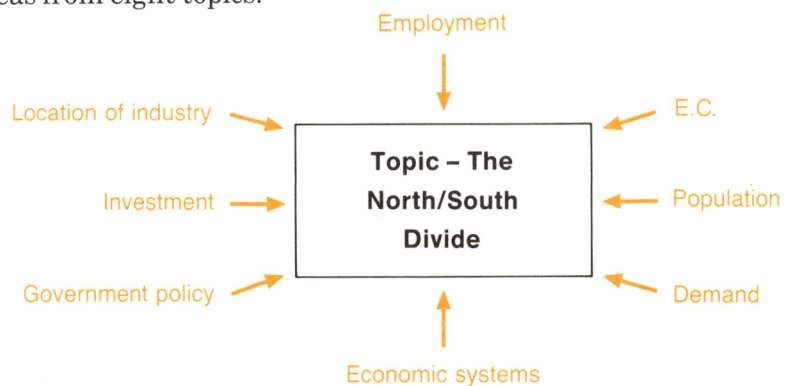

Fig. 5.5 Topics related to the main theme

Within each topic there are also **specific economic concepts** which can be related to your assignment. For instance, the assignment on the 'North–South divide' could use the 'mobility of labour' concept from the 'unemployment' topic. You should also use as many of the **general concepts**, outlined in Section Four, as possible – many of these will feature prominently in your notebook.

This sort of information (including the 'related topics' diagram) should be used in your 'Introduction'.

Textbooks

Reference and textbooks can be useful sources of background secondary information. If you have the time, it is probably a good idea to consult more than one textbook. The different approach and emphasis of another textbook could be useful and your assignment will be marked up as you use more sources. Books other than your usual textbooks may not be available in class, so you may need to visit the **school and public libraries**.

You must use books selectively, so as not to waste time. Ask the **librarians** to help you choose books. Do not try to read whole books! Look at the **chapter headings** and the index. These will give you ideas and perspectives as well as saving time. Do not rely on your memory – **make notes** from what you read. Head your paper (file paper) with the book's title, the author's name and the numbers of the pages used. You will need this information for your **bibliography**. Use a separate sheet of paper for each book you consult.

You should not be afraid to copy out of a textbook. However, again, be very selective. Do not copy out large chunks. Try to choose significant, interesting and (maybe) amusing pieces which are relevant to your assignment. If you use direct **quotes** from books in your final work, make sure you acknowledge the source. Put quotation marks before and after the copied sentence(s) and write the name of the book and the author in brackets after the quote. (If you use a table, put the source of information in brackets under the table.)

The information gathered from textbooks will be used mainly in your 'Introduction'.

Example

The following notes were made from three popular GCSE Economics books for an assignment using the title 'What is the size of the Black Economy and what are the economic consequences?'

> *Allow plenty of time when visiting the library.*

Action Economics – Andrew Leake – 1986

Page 142

The Black Economy is made up of people who earn without paying direct taxes, + pay without paying paying indirect taxes. This is, of course, illegal. Others 'dodge' paying taxes by finding flaws in the tax laws. This doesn't stop them paying taxes at all but it keeps the bill down.

GCSE Economics – Robert Paisley + John Quillfeldt – 1984

Page 216

Transactions made in the black economy are not recorded on National Income Figures.

Letts Revise Economics – Keith West – 1985

Page 4

Illegal trading activity within any economy is know as 'the black economy'. This unofficial Trading can take either:-
'Payments in kind' – One man mends another man's mower in return for having a leak mended.
'Barrow jobs' – jobs done at cheap prices which aren't declared to the govt.

Newspapers

Newspapers are another easily accessible source of information. **Local newspapers** are particularly useful for background information on a **local issue or area study**. Both daily and weekly newspapers can provide relevant material. If your family does not receive or keep these, your friends, neighbours or relatives could probably help you. Sometimes, you need **back copies** of a newspaper. These can usually be found in the 'Reference' section of your local library (ask the librarian).

National daily newspapers may also be valuable sources of information, particularly when you are considering **general economic decisions**. The 'quality' newspapers (e.g. *The Times, The Guardian, The Independent* and *The Daily Telegraph*) each have several pages devoted for financial and economic matters, as well as good coverage of general issues. The *Financial Times* provides a wealth of information and will usually be found in your **school library**, along with one or two of the other newspapers mentioned.

It is important to remember that newspaper articles may be **politically biased**. Recognition of this when you discuss the information you have gathered will improve your marks – it will demonstrate your judgmental skills. You could also refer to the issue of political bias in newspapers in your 'Conclusions' section. Relevant **cuttings** should be taken from newspapers and stored in your folder. They can be included in the 'Appendices' section of your finished assignment. Library newspaper articles will need to be **photocopied**. (Usually there will be a small charge, e.g. 10p.) The major newspapers are quite happy to allow such photocopying for school projects. You do not need to write to ask for permission. Take care to note the date and the name of the newspaper the cutting (or copy) was taken from (again, for your bibliography).

Example

This clipping could be used in a discussion about the privatization of council services. It shows a useful contrast of opinions.

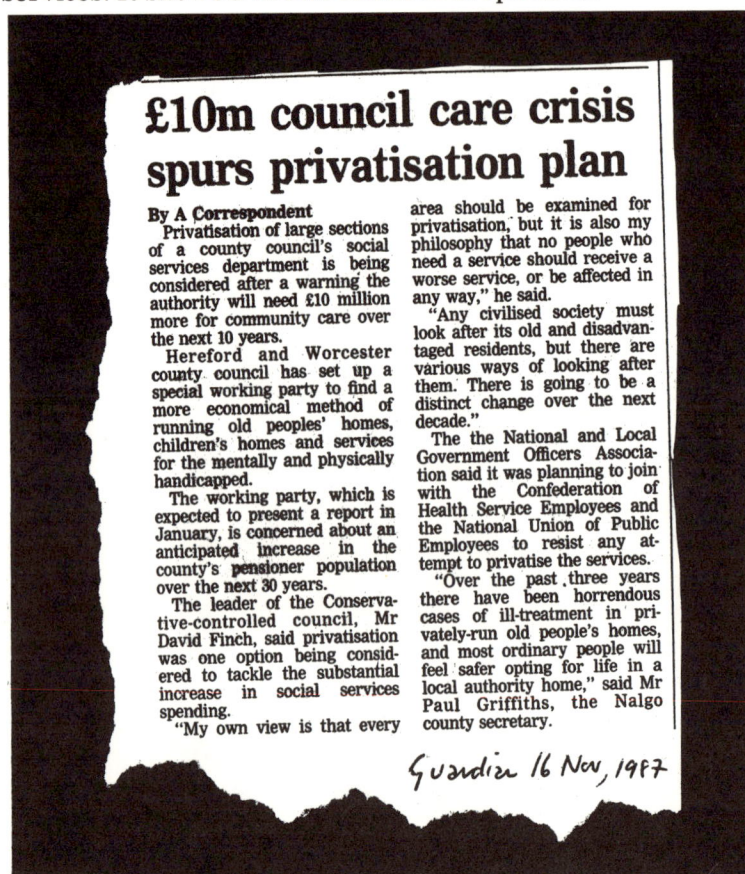

£10m council care crisis spurs privatisation plan

By A Correspondent

Privatisation of large sections of a county council's social services department is being considered after a warning the authority will need £10 million more for community care over the next 10 years.

Hereford and Worcester county council has set up a special working party to find a more economical method of running old peoples' homes, children's homes and services for the mentally and physically handicapped.

The working party, which is expected to present a report in January, is concerned about an anticipated increase in the county's pensioner population over the next 30 years.

The leader of the Conservative-controlled council, Mr David Finch, said privatisation was one option being considered to tackle the substantial increase in social services spending.

"My own view is that every area should be examined for privatisation, but it is also my philosophy that no people who need a service should receive a worse service, or be affected in any way," he said.

"Any civilised society must look after its old and disadvantaged residents, but there are various ways of looking after them. There is going to be a distinct change over the next decade."

The the National and Local Government Officers Association said it was planning to join with the Confederation of Health Service Employees and the National Union of Public Employees to resist any attempt to privatise the services.

"Over the past three years there have been horrendous cases of ill-treatment in privately-run old people's homes, and most ordinary people will feel safer opting for life in a local authority home," said Mr Paul Griffiths, the Nalgo county secretary.

Guardian 16 Nov, 1987

Fig. 5.6 (Reproduced by permission of *The Guardian*.)

Magazines

The Economist, as its name suggests, looks at financial news and general issues from an Economics perspective. It will be available in the public library and possibly the school library.

Specialist magazines are especially valuable when your assignment is based on a hobby or pastime. For example, if you are considering 'The efficiency of advertising of American football in Britain' you would need to examine specialist magazines/newspapers such as 'Touch Down'. Again, if you do not have them at home, or cannot afford to buy them, your local library will keep copies of the more popular specialist magazines.

Again, relevant cuttings (or copies) may need to be collected. Remember to date them and note what magazine they came from and put them in your 'Appendix'. Also, refer to them in your bibliography. Direct quotes from articles should be treated in the same way as quotes from books.

✓ **Checklist – Books, newspapers and magazines**

DO
- read more than your classroom textbook
- make notes from your reading
- be selective
- keep a record of titles, authors, dates, etc
- keep copies of newspaper and magazine articles
- store the notes and clippings safely in your folder

DON'T
- forget the public library
- read whole books
- copy irrelevant material
- try to cram all your notes onto one sheet of paper

Official statistics

Such information is fairly easy to obtain, either directly from the government or local body department who produce it, or from your public library.

The statistics are **reliable** and **accurate**, although **not always up-to-date**. For instance, the data in the most recent edition of *Social Trends* is usually at least one year old. Some local authorities and a few libraries keep '**Small area statistics**' for each (local government) ward. This is 1981 census data on the people in the area concerned. However, it is getting out of date now, and will not be updated until at least 1991.

The other problem is that official figures may not be measured or organized as you want. This is particularly true if you use a general publication to obtain local information.

Example

A student making a comparison between consumer expenditure in South Humberside and London in 1987 found that:

- S. Humberside was not mentioned as an area on its own, but as part of 'Yorkshire and Humberside';

- 'London' was similarly included under the 'South East' heading;

- the most recent data available only went up to 1984. He still used the statistics, but pointed out their limitations, for comparison purposes, in his analysis.

There are many **government publications** which can yield facts and figures. The following publications are usually available for reference in your local public library: *Annual Abstract of Statistics, Economic Trends, Regional Trends* and *Social Trends*.

Consumer Expenditure

			Food, drink + tobacco (m)	Housing + Fuel (m)	Other (m)	Consumer expenditure £/head
1975 →	Yorks/Humb.	£	1,671	0,859	2,601	1,066
	South East	£	6,158	4,282	12,080	1,327
	England	£	16,184	10,102	28,085	1,178
1982 →	Yorks/Humb.	£	3,639	2,690	6,236	2,636
	South East	£	13,897	12,124	31,309	3,384
	England	£	36,118	29,881	72,341	3,003
1983 →	Yorks/Humb.	£	3,859	2,705	7,023	2,853
	South East	£	15,083	13,262	35,407	3,755
	England	£	38,979	31,769	80,703	3,282
1984 →	Yorks/Humb.	£	4,050	2,872	7,694	3,071
	South East	£	16,029	14,104	38,685	4,025
	England	£	41,139	33,532	87,395	3,501

The above chart shows how much the whole of the specified county spends in a year. The end column shows how much each person spends on themselves each year. Each year that is shown, the total consumer expenditure only rises slightly. Although the expenditure for each item rises, on average, twice the amount it rose before. The exception to this is in Yorkshire/Humberside on the Housing and fuel column. This may be because Yorkshire/Humberside's population has been in a depression.

Fig. 5.7 Date collected from *Regional Trends*, a government publication

Example

The government publications just mentioned were scoured for the information by the student comparing Humberside and the South East. He obtained data from *Regional Trends* and analysed it as shown in Figure 5.7 (opposite).

Other government publications, which your teacher may have, are *Economic Progress Report* (published by the Treasury) and *Employment Gazette* (published monthly by the Department of Employment).

When you go to the library take **lined paper**, **pens** and a **ruler** (lined paper and columns help keep your copied data tidy). Research usually takes longer than you expect so give yourself plenty of time. Do not waste time searching aimlessly in the Reference section – ask a **librarian** to help you find the specific information you need.

Again, look carefully at '**Contents' lists** and **headings**. Be very selective – do not copy out lots of figures; keep asking yourself, 'Are these relevant/ useful for my specific topic?' If you copy numbers (from tables or graphs), be careful to **copy accurately** particularly noting the scale of measurement. Figures referring to money are often in billions rather than millions and population figures are often in thousands. Make sure that you **note the source** of the information so that it can be properly acknowledged in your bibliography.

Checklist – Official statistics

DO • use lined paper, and a ruler to keep notes neat
 • use the 'experts' (i.e. the librarians)
 • carefully note table headings
 • check the scale of measurement

DON'T • copy irrelevant material
 • forget to note the source of the information

Presentation of data

The way in which your data is presented is most important. The syllabuses of most examination groups actually specify that assignment marks are to be given for presentation:

> 'Materials fully and clearly explained and a good range of presentation skills demonstrated. Full use of appropriate economic terminology: up to 5/25 marks.' (*SEG syllabus*)

Use a variety of presentation techniques.

Collection and presentation of relevant data is particularly emphasized in the MEG syllabus. Teachers are instructed to allocate up to 15 marks out of 40 to these skills.

In general, data should be presented next to or above the comments which interpret and analyse it. You may wish to present some data (e.g. a large table or graph) on a separate sheet. This is perfectly acceptable, but when you number the pages when you finish the project (see 'List of contents' in Section Eight) make sure that the data and the related comments are on consecutive pages. You should not present all the data together, as it will make organization and understanding of the data difficult. Each piece of data should be **numbered** (e.g. table 1, table 2, . . .). This enables easy reference within the text. Each piece should also be given a **title**.

There are many methods which can be used to present data. You might be able to use skills developed in other subjects. For instance, Information Technology might enable you to use a computer graphics package to illustrate your data.

For each method presented here, I will describe the method, explain what it is used for and why it might be preferable to others and give some examples. Most importantly, a list of **conventions** will be given for each method. These are the construction rules for the particular format.

Methods for numerical data

Tables of figures

Tables with several rows and columns of statistics usually give a lot of information. They can be used to present the **whole picture** of something. You will find them most useful when **summarizing data** collected from surveys and official statistics. Tables of figures are usually featured at the start of the 'Analysis' section. The table shown below (table 6.1) is fairly simple, compared to some which can be constructed. It shows the results of a survey of newspaper advertisements for second-hand Sierra cars, with reference to the main selling points stressed in the advertisements.

Example

Table 6.1 Sierra car advertising features

Registration letter (year)	D	C	B	A	Others	Total
Numbers of ads mentioning: colour condition mileage	7 0 7	1 1 1	1 2 0	8 1 2	4 0 0	21 4 10
Total	14	3	3	11	4	35

Tables can show **many interrelationships**. There is therefore a danger that the reader will not be able to 'see the wood for the trees'. If you wish to concentrate on a few specific aspects, pictorial methods, such as histograms, might be better.

Conventions

1 Tables should be **boxed**, with **straight (ruled) lines** dividing rows and columns as necessary.

2 The table and all its columns should be **clearly labelled**.

3 The table should have a **title** which summarizes the subject of data.

4 If the table includes 'totals', (as in table 6.1), make sure that:
(a) the grand total is accurate – Check that you get the same number adding across-the-row and down the column totals.
(b) if you use percentages, that they add up to 100. Sometimes, with official statistics, rounding up or down gives totals of 99 or 101 per cent as in the next example (table 6.2).

5 When using **official statistics** or other people's figures (e.g. from newspapers) name the **source** of the information and the **date** of the publication.

Example

In the following example, data on modes of transport was simplified slightly.

Table 6.2 Transport to and from work, by main mode of transport

| | Main mode (percentages) | | | | | | |
	Rail	Bus	Car, van, lorry	Motor-cycle	Bicycle	Walk	Other
1965	6	32	35	4	12	8	2
1972–3	5	23	54	3	6	6	3
1978–9	5	19	59	3	5	7	3
1985–6	5	11	67	3	6	6	2

(*Source: National Travel Survey, Department of Transport Social Trends, 1988, p. 149*)

Histograms

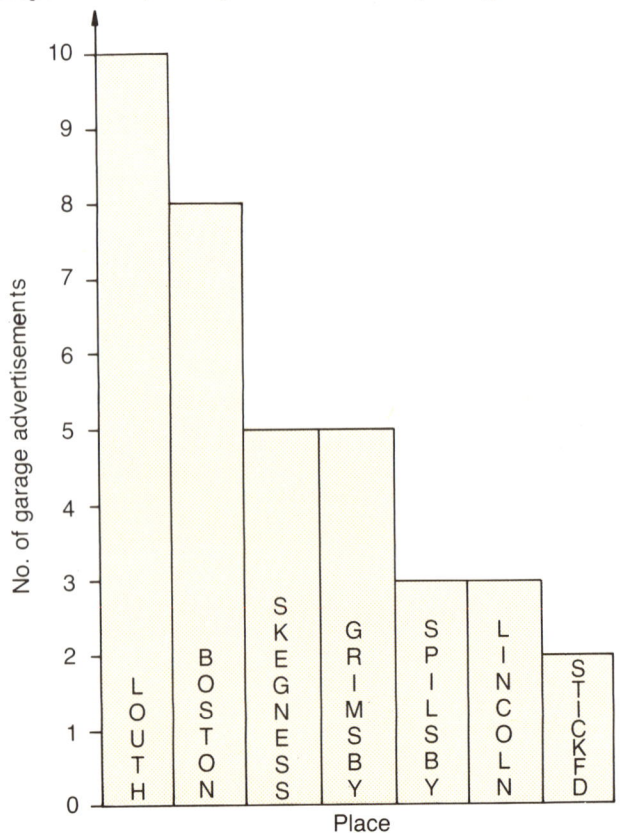

Fig. 6.1 A histogram showing places with more than one garage advertising

Histograms are also called **bar charts**. They use **lines** and **levels** for measurement. Histograms can be used to show the results of **simple counting exercises**. The example on the previous page, Figure 6.1, shows the number of garages in certain Lincolnshire towns and villages advertising cars for sale in a local newspaper.

Histograms can be used to show **relative sizes** of items in a group of things. They stress the highest and lowest (largest and smallest). For instance, in Figure 6.1, it is clear that more garages in Louth than in Boston advertise in this local newspaper.

More complex histograms can be devised where two different sets of data relating to the same phenomenon are shown simultaneously. The bars of the histogram can be shaded or coloured for effect. The next example (Figure 6.2) illustrates similar data collected on two different occasions.

Example

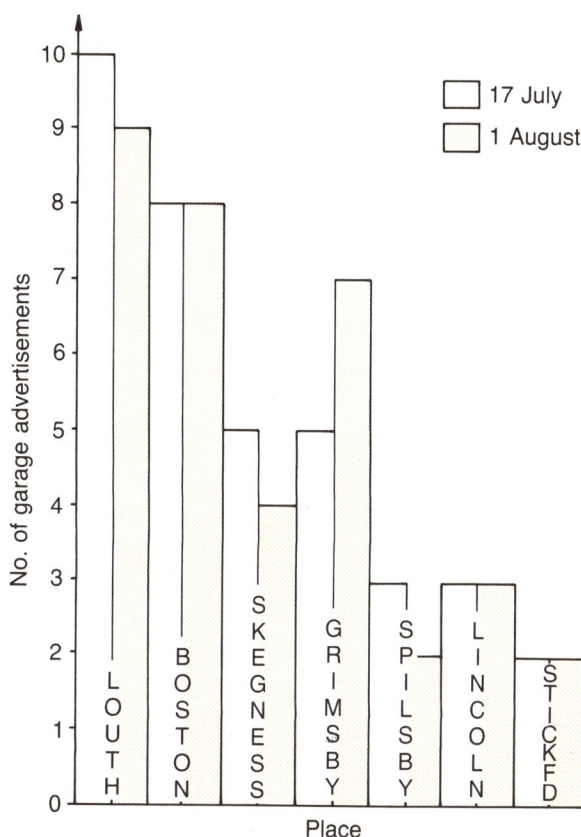

Fig. 6.2 Garage advertising on two occasions

Conventions

1 Choose a scale of measurement which enables you to show your results clearly. In the garage advertising survey histograms (Figures 6.1 and 6.2), it was sensible to measure in single units. If you are dealing with larger numbers, this will be impractical.

2 If your histogram is in the body of the text, as the examples in this book are, rather than on separate sheets, try not to exceed **half a page** in size.

3 It is usual for the scale of measurement (the **numbers**) to be on the **vertical axis**.

4 It is easier to draw and scale on **lined paper**. (You could also use graph paper.)

5 **Label** both axes clearly and give the histogram a **title**.

6 Provide a **clear, accurate key**, if more than one set of data is being shown (e.g. Figure 6.2).

7 If you have sufficient space and/or only a few items, leave (equal) spaces between the columns.

Pictograms

Pictograms (or pictographs) are a form of histogram which uses **pictorial symbols** to represent size and/or number. They provide an opportunity to show your artistic flair, but choose pictures which are appropriate and easy to draw, otherwise the pictogram will detract from rather than enhance your work.

An interesting difference between histograms and pictograms is that the scale of measurement on pictograms is usually given on the horizontal axis.

Example

A survey was made of traffic levels in a high street on different days of a week. The statistics collected were illustrated by a pictogram with each symbol representing 100 cars. The exact total for each day was placed at the end of each row.

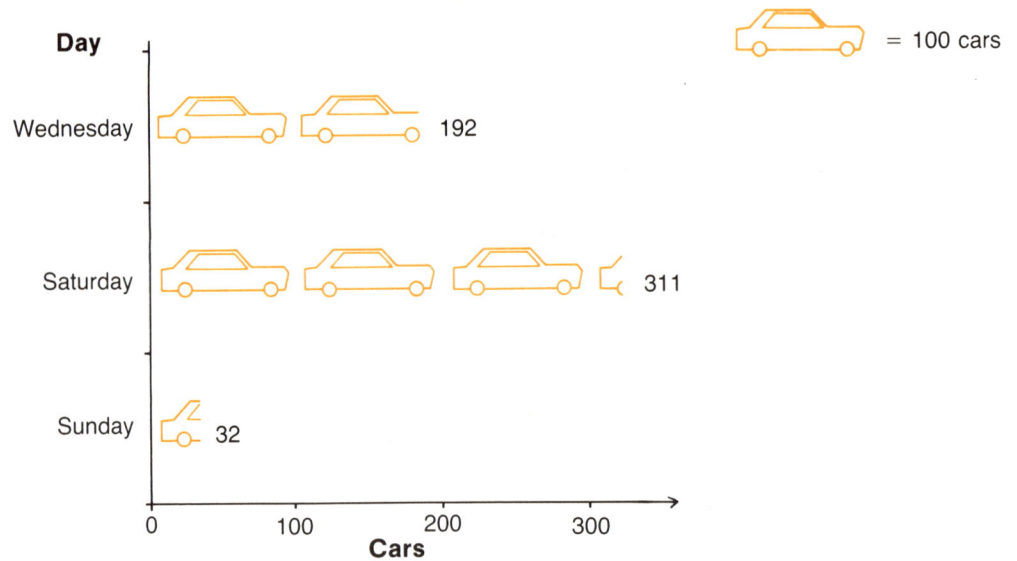

Fig. 6.3 A pictogram showing the number of cars counted on selected days

Conventions

As for histograms rules 1–6, except that numbers are usually on the horizontal axis.

1 Make symbols simple and appropriate to the subject.

2 Give a scale or key to represent what each symbol represents.

3 Make sure all full symbols are the same size.

4 Use part of a symbol to represent data which is less than the full scale size.

5 Space the symbols evenly.

Pie charts

These are circles ('pies') which are subdivided into segments ('slices') representing the different items in a group. They demonstrate the **relative importance** of the items, compared to the whole. In the following example (Figure 6.4, next page) the data from the first histogram example (Figure 6.1) is represented in pie chart form.

Pie charts are a more sophisticated method of presentation than histograms. In the histogram example (Figure 6.1) the actual number of garages in each place was shown. Since the segments of a pie chart represent fractions of the whole data, the amounts are usually expressed as **percentages** – in this example, the percentage of the total number of garage advertisements.

Example

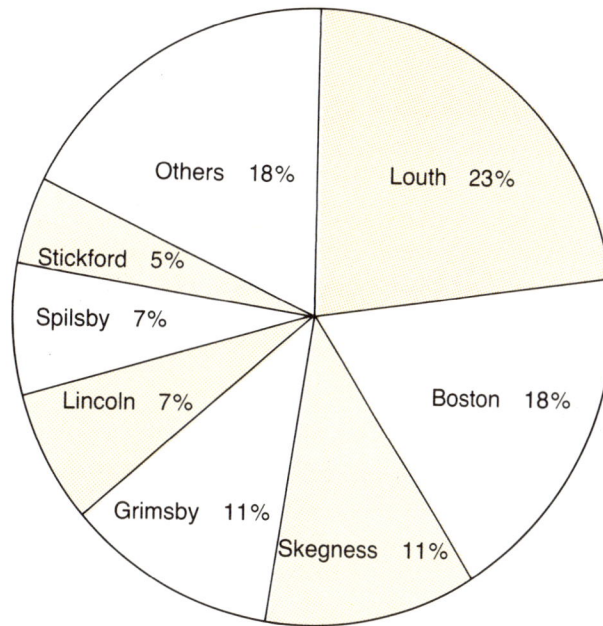

Fig. 6.4 Location of garages advertising in a local newspaper

Another difference to notice is that the pie chart includes an **'Others'** category. The histogram only showed results for places with more than one garage advertising (a total of 36 garages). In fact, 44 garages advertised in the newspaper surveyed – 8 (18 per cent) towns had only garage advertising so were ignored on the histogram. These have to be included in the pie chart which represents the whole data. Rather than having eight very small segments, these relatively unimportant items are brought together in the 'Others' category.

Unless you use a large circle, it is often difficult to label inside the portions clearly. You can overcome this difficulty by shading the portions in different colours or patterns and providing a key.

If the total figure is quite small, percentage shares can be misleading, so pie charts should be avoided for small samples.

Conventions

1 Use a pair of **compasses** to draw your circle.

2 Find the percentage of the whole represented by each segment, i.e.

$$\frac{\text{number shown by segment}}{\text{total data}} \times 100\%$$

In the garages example, Louth garages placed 10 of the total of 44 advertisements, i.e.

$$\frac{10}{44} \times 100\% \approx 23\%$$

3 Find the angle for each segment by calculating the fraction of the whole circle (360 degrees), i.e.

$$\frac{\text{number shown by segment}}{\text{total data}} \times 360°$$

In the garages example, the segment for Louth garages should measure approximately $82° \left(\frac{10}{44} \times 360 \right)$. Check the angle on Figure 6.4.

4 Imagine that your circle is a clockface and draw your first line from the centre to 12 o'clock.

5 Use a **protractor** to measure and draw the angle of each segment at the centre of the circle.

6 Neatly **label each segment**. If the labels will not fit inside a segment, place it outside with an arrow to the area. Alternatively, you could shade each segment and provide a key.

7 Give the pie chart a suitable **title**.

Graphs

Graphs are more sophisticated than histograms and pie charts. They are used when you wish to illustrate a relationship between **two or more variables**. When the relationship is plotted on a graph, a **general trend** can be identified, as can any **deviations** from the general trend.

Graphs are particularly used to illustrate changes that occur over periods of **time**. On such graphs 'time' is the label for the horizontal axis.

Example

Figure 6.5(a) is a **line graph** showing the relationship between the age and average price of a secondhand car. You will notice that the average price falls with age (the 'trend') but not in a clearly predictable way ('deviation').

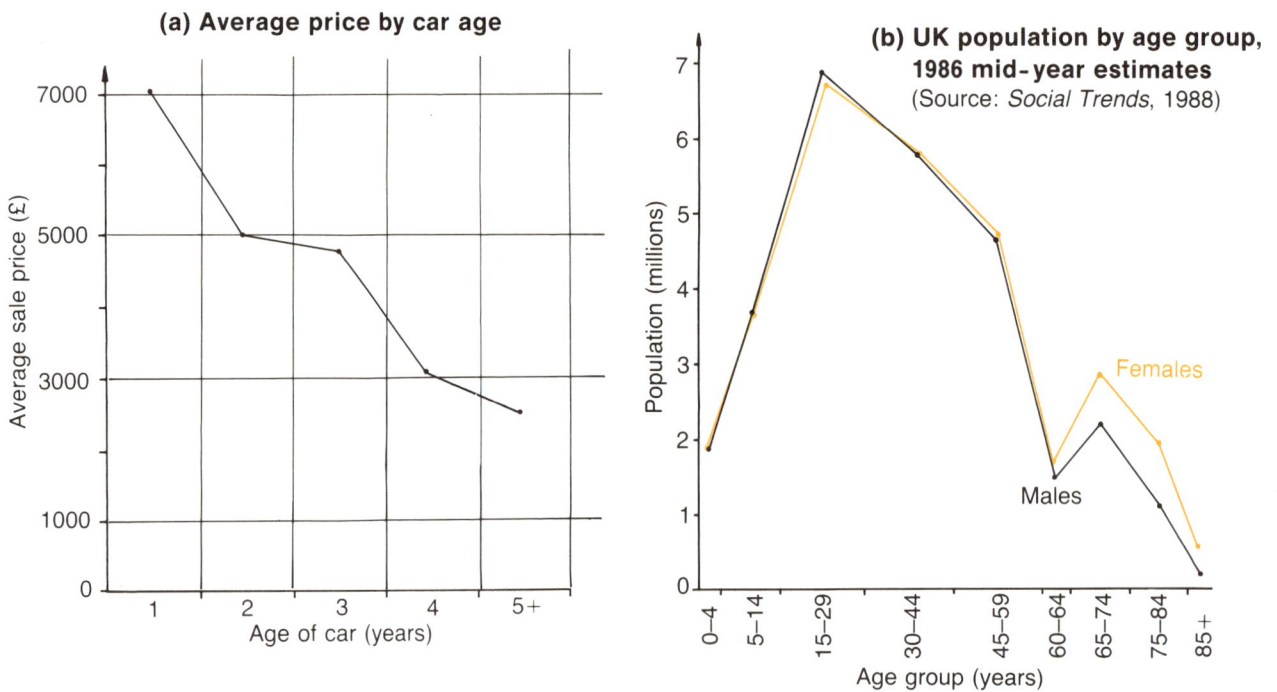

Fig. 6.5 Line graphs

Sometimes several relationships may be plotted on the same graph. For instance, the graphs of male and female population by age group could be shown on the same graph (see Figure 6.5(b)). Sex differences in employment, leisure time, qualifications, etc., could be plotted similarly.

Generally, it is advisable to plot a maximum of three lines (relationships) on one graph, because the lines may cross each other making the diagram less clear. If you include graphs in your assignment you should explain the trends and deviations in the Analysis section, giving possible reasons.

Conventions

As for histograms, rules 1–6.

Methods for non-numerical data

Diagrams

A diagram is simply a drawing which explains or can be used to explain something for example, a sketch, a plan or a graph. The usual idea is to simplify a complicated pattern. The diagrams we have seen so far have all represented numerical data. Perhaps the most useful application in assignment work for diagrams showing non-numerical data is to summarize a complex organization, for example, the organizational framework of a business and the number of employees in each department as shown in Figure 6.6.

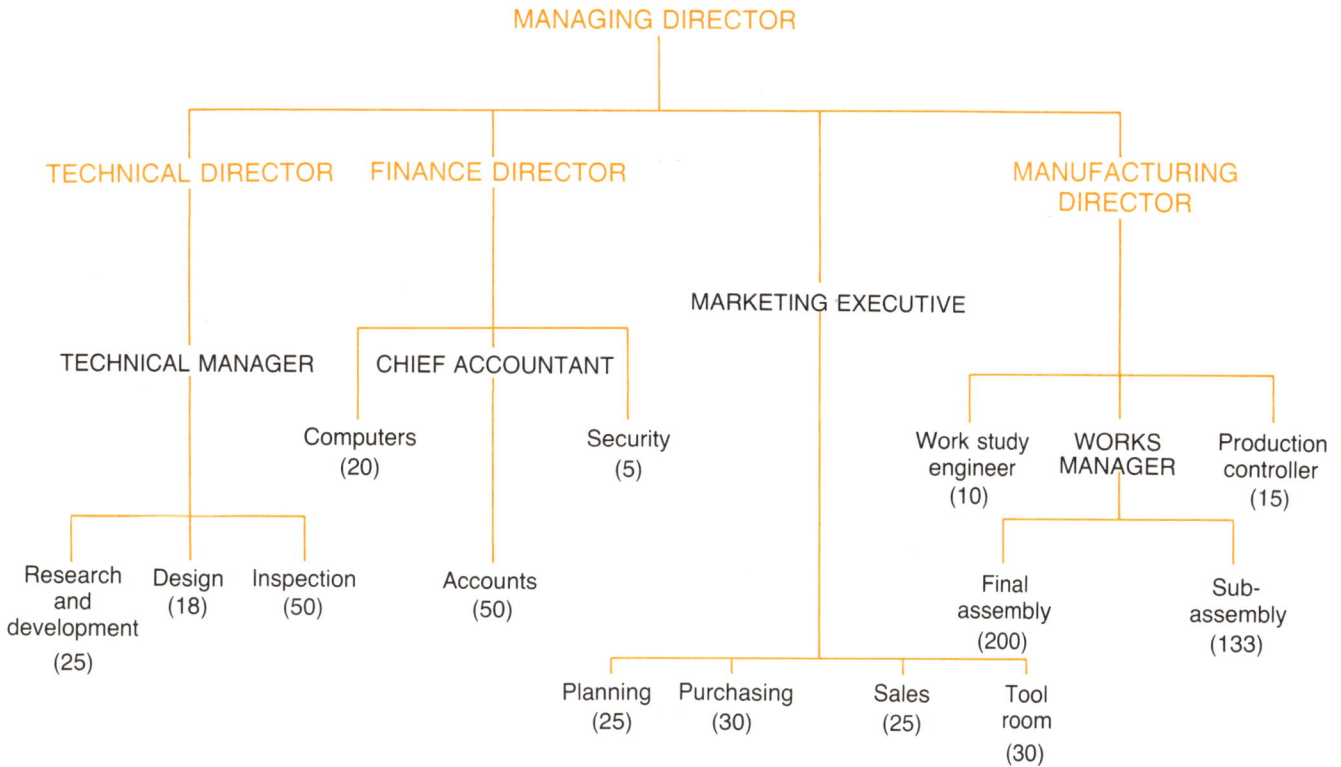

Fig. 6.6 A diagram illustrating the organizational structure of a manufacturing company

Conventions

1 Before starting to draw, consider the **extent** of the diagram in width and length. Once again, if the diagram is going to be within the text, try not to exceed half a page in size.

2 Always make a draft (practice) sketch.

3 Print labels clearly alongside the relevant lines.

Flow charts

Flow charts are used to show **progressions** and **interrelationships**. They show the **links** between different variables. At a simple descriptive level, a flow chart can illustrate a **chain of events**. They may also indicate a decision-making process or **'cause and effect'**.

Example

In the business hierarchy illustrated in Figure 6.6, the chain of command between the managing director and a salesman could be described by a flow chart as shown here (Figure 6.7). A vertical 'slice' of the organization has been taken.

Flow charts can be more complicated with **loops** and **feedback** (as in computer programming). The size of the boxes can also be varied to show the relative importance of the items.

Conventions

1 Prepare a rough practice sketch.

2 Write out the longest labels first, to work out the necessary size of the boxes.

3 They must be **large enough** to include legibly printed words. Draw boxes with pencil and **ruler**.

Fig. 6.7

Maps

Maps can be useful in setting a **context** for your assignment. The best assignments are usually very specific pieces of research. For example, if you were looking at 'the local market for secondhand cars' (MEG prescribed title, 1988) you need carefully to define 'local' in the geographical area you are considering.

Maps should **not** be **too detailed**. They should stress the theme which is being illustrated. In the following example, (from the assignment on secondhand car advertising), the main places with garages advertising cars in the newspaper considered were featured.

Example

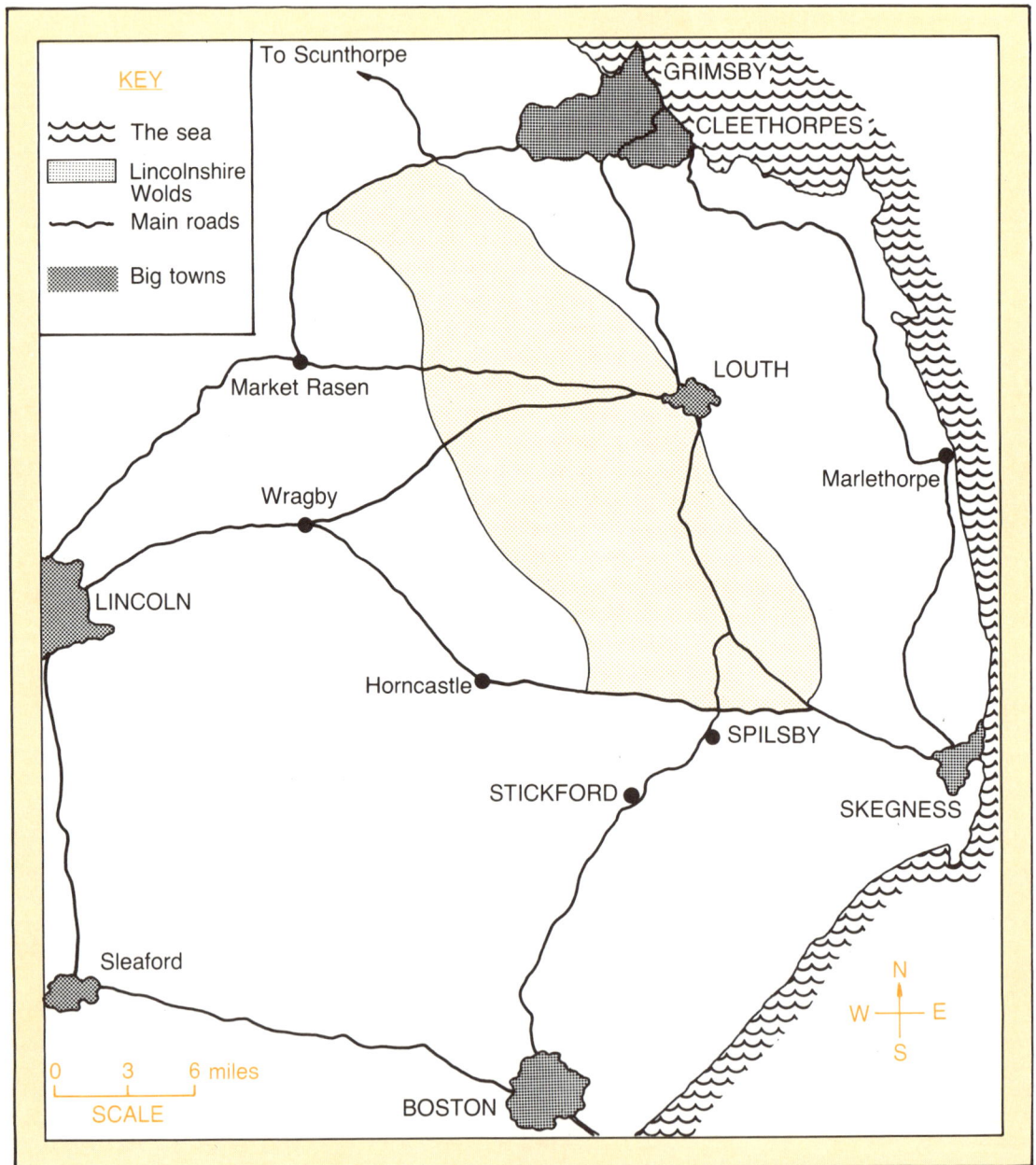

Fig. 6.8 Map showing the local region around Louth

Rather than put too much information on one map, it is sometimes better to draw separate maps and then make comparisons. For instance, it would be useful to compare newspaper circulation in the geographical areas concerned when considering placement of secondhand car advertisements (even though the boundaries of the two maps might be different).

Conventions

1 Plan the **size** of map needed in rough.

2 Maps can be made **colourful** but they should not be garish, i.e. avoid very bright, vivid colours. Realistic colours should be used where appropriate e.g. rivers and the sea in blue.

3 Colours should be used consistently and a **key** provided.

4 Always include a **compass indicating North** and a **scale**.

5 Put the map in a **frame**.

✓ Checklist

DO
- use a range of presentation methods
- give each figure a title
- write clearly – print or use block capitals
- number each figure – Figure 1, Figure 2, etc

DON'T
- rush into drawing, without rough practice sketches
- make figures bigger than half a page
- forget scales, keys, labels, as appropriate
- keep your diagrams isolated from the text

Application and analysis of data

Terms and concepts

Key economic concepts

As the coursework assessment objectives show, you need to use economic terms and ideas in a relevant way. You must first be aware of the **central (or 'key') economic concepts**. As specified in many textbooks, the most important are:

- **Scarcity**
- **Choice**
- **Opportunity cost**
- **Interdependence**
- **Efficiency**

The general nature of these concepts is such that they can be **applied to any, and every**, piece of economics coursework.

Example

In an assignment about the use of part-time staff, you can consider:

- The shortage of staff (**scarcity**) at certain times of week.
- The employers **choice** between full-time and part-time staff.
- The **opportunity cost** of any staffing decision.
- The need for cooperation between all staff, particularly two half-time (job-sharing) staff, i.e. **interdependence**.
- The **efficient** use of full-time and part-time staff.

Concept networks

There are many other economic terms and much knowledge which can be **applied selectively**. **Concept networks** for the most popular assignment themes (outlined in Section Four), are given here, showing relevant economic ideas which could be featured in assignments (Figures 7.1 – 7.5).

Examples

1 **Case study** e.g. local shop

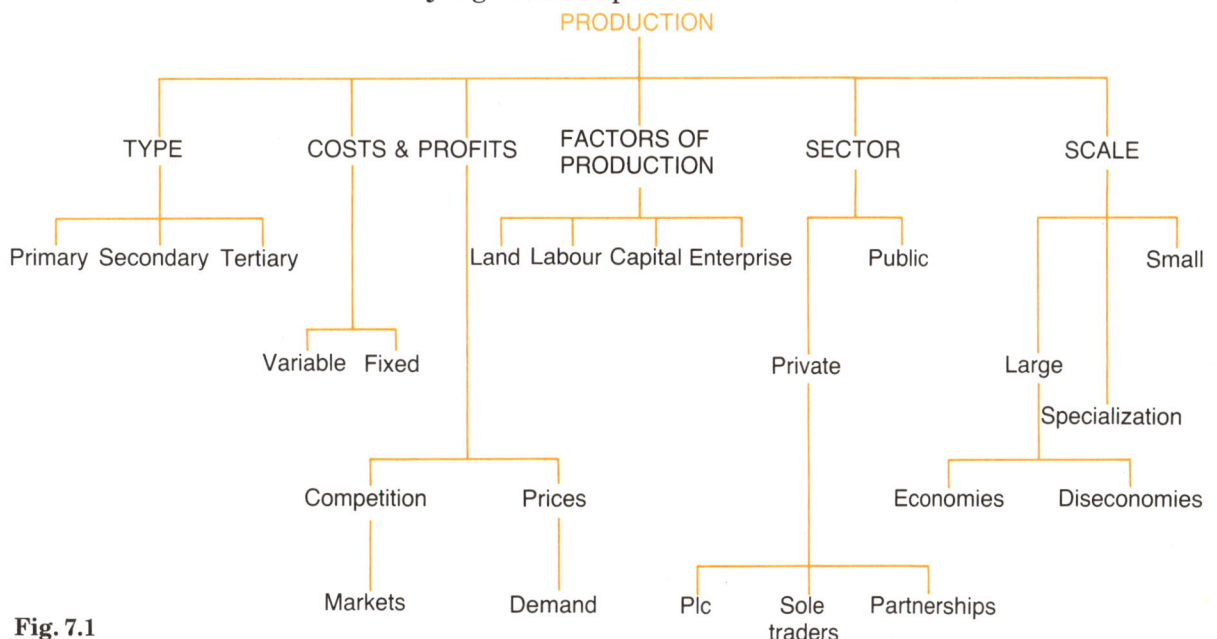

Fig. 7.1

2 Local issue e.g. factory closure

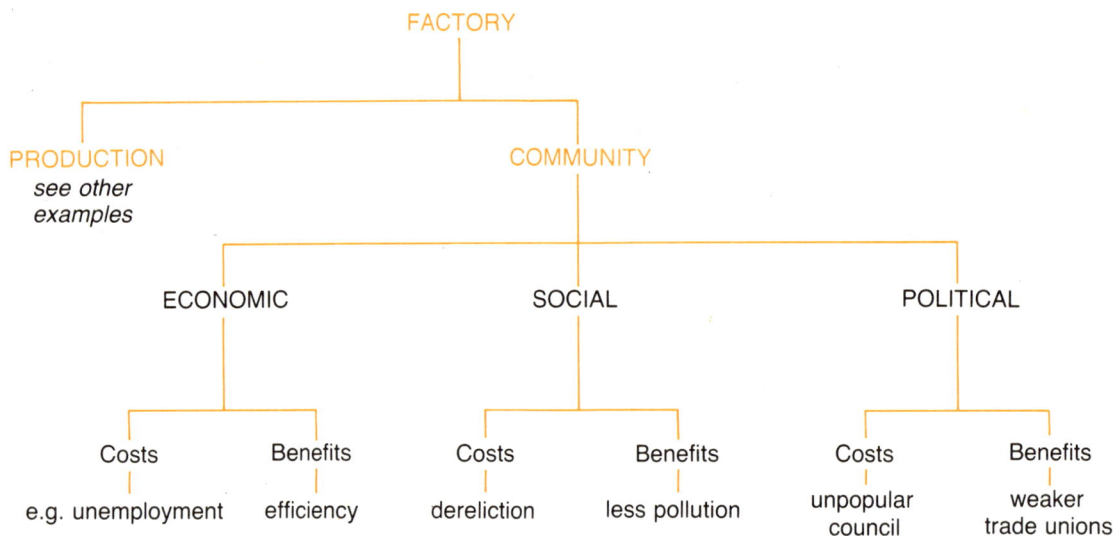

```
                            FACTORY
                               |
         ┌─────────────────────┴──────────────────────┐
     PRODUCTION                                    COMMUNITY
    see other                                          |
    examples              ┌─────────────────┬──────────────────────┐
                       ECONOMIC           SOCIAL                POLITICAL
                          |                 |                        |
                    ┌─────┴─────┐     ┌─────┴─────┐          ┌───────┴───────┐
                  Costs      Benefits Costs     Benefits    Costs         Benefits
                    |           |       |           |         |               |
              e.g. unemployment efficiency dereliction less pollution unpopular   weaker
                                                                     council   trade unions
```

Fig. 7.2

3 National problem e.g. deindustrialization

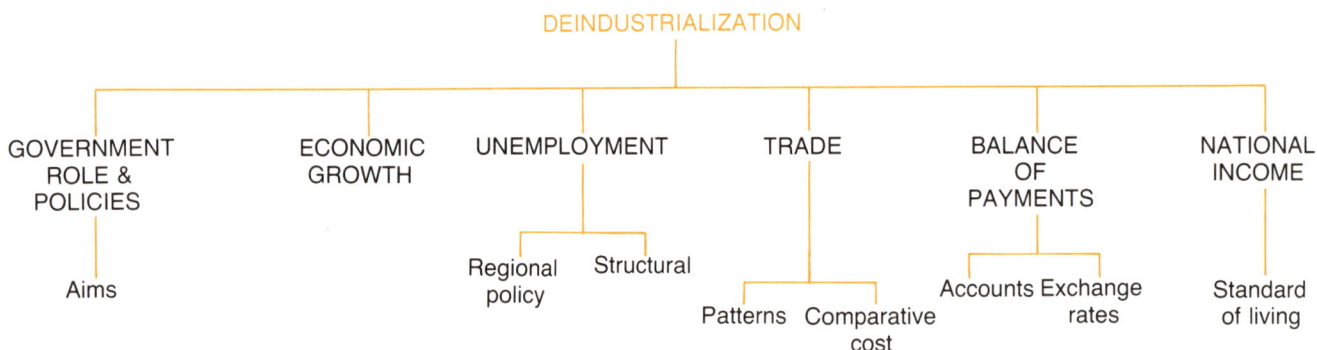

```
                          DEINDUSTRIALIZATION
                                   |
   ┌──────────┬──────────┬─────────┴─────────┬─────────────┬──────────────┐
GOVERNMENT  ECONOMIC  UNEMPLOYMENT        TRADE        BALANCE       NATIONAL
ROLE &      GROWTH                                       OF          INCOME
POLICIES                                              PAYMENTS
   |                      |                  |            |              |
  Aims              ┌─────┴─────┐      ┌─────┴─────┐  ┌────┴────┐        |
                 Regional   Structural Patterns Comparative Accounts Exchange Standard
                 policy                         cost              rates   of living
```

Fig. 7.3

4 Personal decision-making e.g. buying on credit

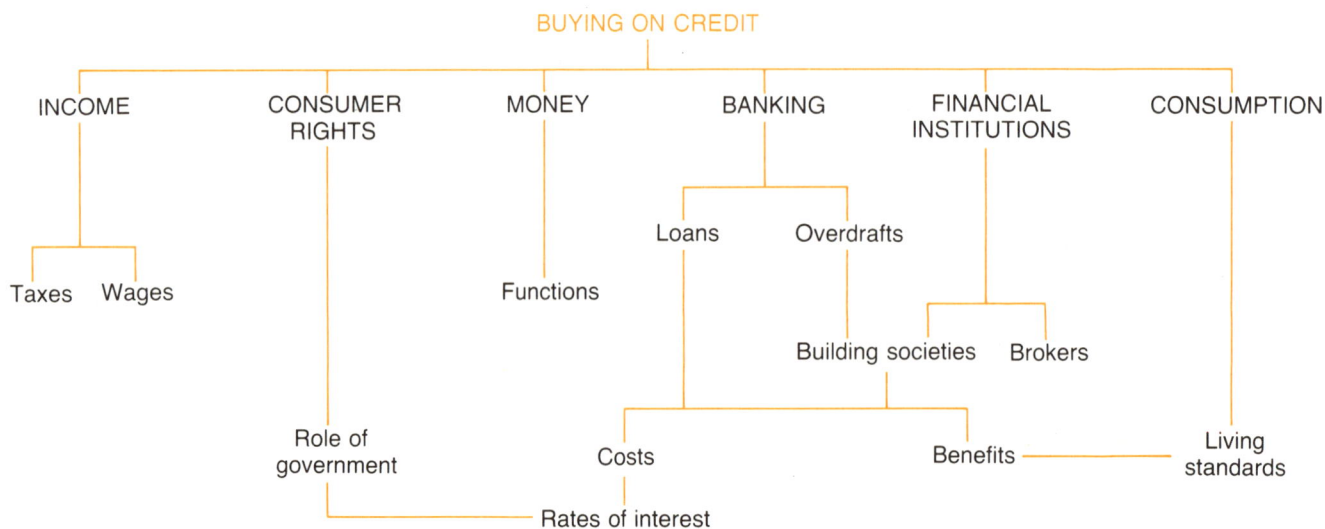

```
                          BUYING ON CREDIT
                                 |
  ┌────────┬──────────┬─────────┴────────┬─────────────────┬──────────────┐
INCOME  CONSUMER    MONEY           BANKING          FINANCIAL       CONSUMPTION
        RIGHTS                                       INSTITUTIONS
  |                    |          ┌──────┴──────┐          |               |
┌─┴──┐                Functions Loans      Overdrafts  ┌───┴────┐          |
Taxes Wages                                        Building   Brokers      |
                                                   societies                |
        |                          |                    |                   |
     Role of                     Costs              Benefits ──────── Living
     government                     |                                 standards
        |                           |
        └──────────────── Rates of interest
```

Fig. 7.4

5 Area study e.g. village survey

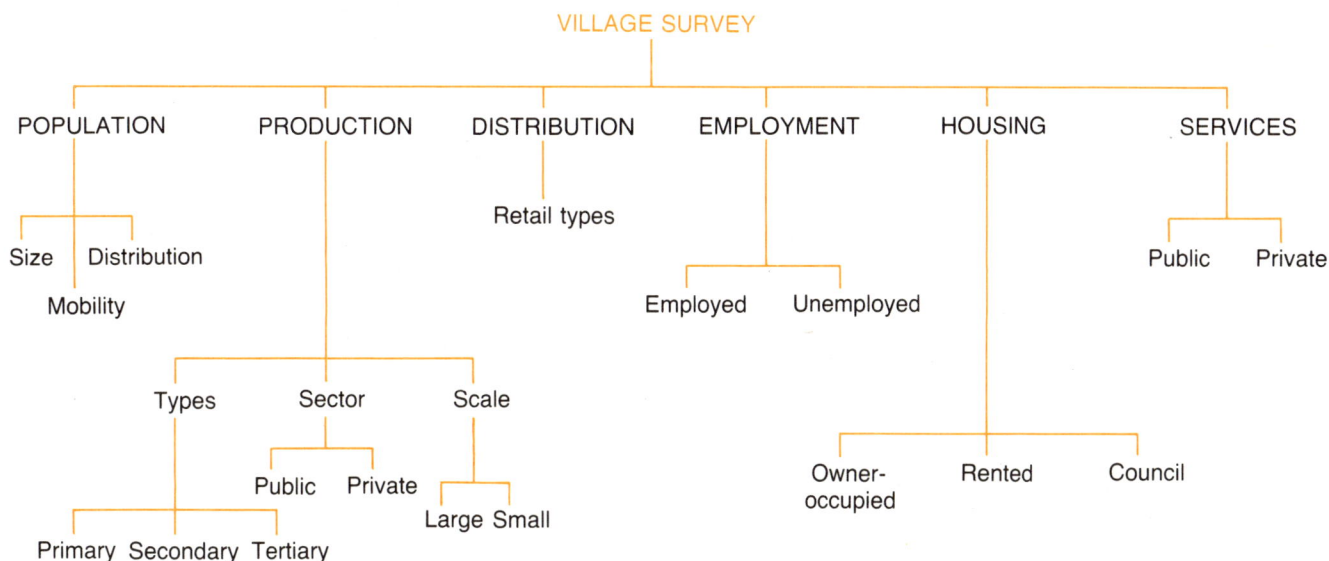

Fig. 7.5

Application of concepts

You should try to bring relevant concepts into your 'Introduction'. If you use the key words in your title, as suggested in Section Four, you will have several starting points. Quite a few words in the title will give you more scope for comment. Make a list of all the concepts and ideas which you think could be relevant. Your initial list of concepts and ideas could be expanded by referring to the relevant chapters in your textbook and your notebook. The five examples (Figures 7.1 – 7.5) were prepared in that way.

Application involves relating the concepts and ideas to your problem. Start with your list of concepts and ideas. Consider each important principle in turn and decide whether it is particularly relevant to your problem. If not, discard it. If you decide it is relevant, you should be able to explain its significance. In the following example you can see how the process develops from the title, to key words, expanding to a list of concepts and, finally, into an opening paragraph.

Example

Title – What factors influence the secondhand car market?

Key words – market, car, secondhand, factors

Concepts – scarcity, choice, opportunity cost, interdependence, efficiency, firm, industry, monopoly, perfect competition, oligopoly, imperfect competition, large scale, small scale, role of Government, retail, wholesale, geographical, primary, secondary, tertiary, economies of scale, public sector, private sector, capital goods, consumer goods.

Opening paragraph –

Cars are part of the wider **industry** of motor vehicles, which is largely in the **private sector**. They are expensive, **consumer durable goods**. Nearly all new cars are sold by **retail** garages. **Secondhand** cars differ from new cars in that many are sold by private individuals. There are many different types of **market** in economic theory, ranging from **perfect competition** through to **monopoly**. In this case we are considering a **local**, rather than a **national**, market. The secondhand car market is one in which there is a lot of **choice**, much advertising, great product **differentiation**. Non-price **factors** may also be important. We will examine both **demand** and **supply** aspects, and hope to establish which market model best describes the secondhand car market.

You will notice that about a third of the ideas in the concepts list have been used in the opening paragraph. Three other economic concepts also appeared in the paragraph although they did not feature in the list (differentiation, demand and supply). The actual writing triggered off **additional ideas**. This often happens. Sometimes you will have to rewrite your introduction to incorporate these extra ideas. It is worth it if the overall quality is improved.

✓ Checklist

DO
- consider the key words of your title
- use the general concepts
- refer to your notes and your textbook
- think about your problem
- prepare a concept network
- apply specific concepts where relevant

DON'T
- be afraid to use jargon
- try to use every concept
- expect to write a perfect introduction first time

Organizing data

Making sense of primary data

The data to be interpreted may be either your own (primary) or someone else's (secondary), or a mixture of the two types. Secondary data is usually in a condensed and manageable form when you collect it. Primary data will probably need to be organized before it can be interpreted. Therefore, before considering the skills of interpretation (analysis), we will look at the organization and simplification of the data which you have collected.

If you have conducted a **survey** you will have probably at least 20 completed questionnaires containing a lot of information. You need to condense this information to manageable proportions on a **master sheet** (or sheets). This will save you having to look through all the completed questionnaires each time you want to check something.

Coding

The first task is to code the data. This means simplifying the survey data by grouping the respondents' answers into categories which can be quickly and easily recorded. Coding is abbreviating the information.

Each completed **questionnaire** should be **numbered**. If your sample has been stratified into different groups, make sure that all the answers from each group are kept together.

Example

If you have stratified your sample by age with 3 groups of 10 people, then the questionnaires from one group should be numbered 1 – 10, from the second group 11 – 20 and from the third group 21 – 30.

If your survey is stratified by two variables, e.g. age and sex, then within each big group you should **keep sub-groups together**.

Example

If the 30 people in the previous example were also divided by sex (15 male and 15 female), code the questionnaires of the male respondents 1 – 15 and make sure that 1 – 5 are one age group, 6 – 10 another and 11 – 15 the third.

Give each **question** in the survey a code to distinguish it from other questions (e.g. Q1, Q2, etc). The **specific answers** given to the questions also need to be coded in a suitable way. Use either letters and/or numbers as appropriate. **Closed questions** are **easier** to code **than open** questions, because you only have a limited number of possible answers.

Yes/no questions are the easiest to codify because you can use 'Y' for yes and 'N' for no.

For **open questions** the following technique works well: Glance through the sheets and get a rough idea of what answers have been given. Make a **list** of all the different answers given and devise a code accordingly. Use an 'others' category for rare answers.

Example

Question:

Where would you look for information on secondhand cars?

Answers:

No.1 Local paper, *Auto Weekly*
No.2 *Grimsby Evening Telegraph*, garages
No.3 Don't know
No.4 Local paper, *Target*
No.5 Garages, local paper

Answer list:

local paper, weekly paper, garages, don't know, magazines.

Codes:

L, W, G, DK, M, O (O = others)

In the above example, the code was based on **inital letters**. This is a good method because it is easy to remember the code when classifying, so you are less likely to make a mistake.

Sometimes it is necessary to invent a **scoring system** to judge answers to factual questions.

Example

A student trying to judge the effectiveness of football sponsorship designed a question to test people's ability to associate a sponsor with a particular team. (One completed copy of the actual questionnaire used in the survey is shown in Figure 7.6, overleaf. We are considering question 3). Instead of coding each individual answer, he noted the number of correct associations (the respondent's 'score') in the relevant column of his master sheet.

The master sheet

Design your master sheet. The first column should show the survey sheet number and in the next column(s) record the characteristics of the respondent (sex, age, etc). The first row should give brief headings for the categories and the questions. In the second row, give keys for your answer codes.

Example

Survey sheet number	Sex	Age	Qn 1 Shop by mail-order?	Qn 2 Which catalogue?	Etc
	M = male F = female	a = U18 b = 19−50 c = 51+	Y = yes N = no	L = Littlewoods G = Grattans K = Kays F = Freemans E = Empire O = Other	
1 2 3 etc					

FOOTBALL SURVEY

AGE: | 15under | | 15 - 40 ✓ | | 40 + | SEX: male ✓
                                                female ☐

1. Name the first football team sponsor which comes into your head:

   SHARP

2. What team do you support?   HALIFAX (Not Liverpool)

3. What football teams have these as a sponsor?

   WANG: OLDHAM ✗   Draper Tools: SOUTH HAMPTON ✓
   AVCO: WOLVES ✗   IVECO: WEST HAM ✗
   JVC: ARSENAL ✓   SHARP: MANCHESTER UNITED ✓
   NEC: EVERTON ✓   BEDFORD: LUTON ✓

   5/8

4. What makes of football trainers can you think of?

   GOLA   HITEC
   DIADORA   REEBOK
   ADIDAS   NIKE

5. When buying football gear, which of the following is most important? (Tick one box)

   A   brand name   ☐
   B   price   ☑
   C   fit   ☐

Fig. 7.6

The completed master sheet shown in Figure 7.7 below summarizes the answers collected in the regional preference survey given as an example in Section Five (see Figure 5.4). The master sheet contains the basic information in the summary form. It is easy to see that although the sample was stratified it was not balanced – there are significantly fewer respondents in the age 41–65 and 65+ age groups. From a completed master sheet you can **quickly and easily identify responses** made by each person in the sample.

For example, the third respondent is the one whose completed questionnaire was shown in Figure 5.4:

  –he is a male student under the age of 18
  –his family own a dishwasher, deep freeze, telephone and a car
  –he likes living in Humberside and would not prefer anywhere else, particularly not the South East

Refer back to Figure 5.4 and check these facts.

| Age | | | | Sex | Emp? | Utl | Like Humb? | Other area? | Like S.E.? |
U18	19–40	41–65	65+	M/F	Y/N/St	1–4	Y/N	Y/N	Y/N/?
★				M	St	234	Y	Y	Y
★				M	St	234	N	Y	Y
★				M	St	1234	Y	N	N
★				M	St	1234	Y	Y	Y
★				M	St	34	Y	Y	Y
★				M	St	1234	Y	Y	Y
★				M	St	34	Y	Y	?
★				M	St	34	N	Y	Y
★				M	St	34	N	Y	N
★				F	St	234	Y	N	N
★				M	Y	23	N	Y	N
★				F	Y	3	Y	N	N
★				F	Y	234	Y	N	N
	★			M	Y	34	Y	Y	N
	★			M	Y	234	N	Y	N
	★			M	Y	1234	N	Y	Y
	★			M	N	3	Y	N	N
	★			M	N	34	N	Y	N
	★			F	Y	34	Y	Y	N
	★			F	Y	1234	Y	N	N
	★			F	Y	34	Y	Y	Y
	★			F	Y	1234	N	Y	N
	★			F	Y	1234	N	Y	Y
	★			F	Y	1234	Y	Y	N
	★			F	Y	234	Y	N	N
	★			F	Y	23	N	Y	Y
	★			F	Y	234	Y	N	N
	★			F	N	234	Y	N	N
	★			F	N	1234	Y	Y	Y
		★		M	Y	34	Y	Y	Y
		★		M	Y	234	?	Y	N
		★		M	Y	234	Y	N	N
		★		F	Y	234	Y	Y	N
		★		F	Y	1234	Y	N	N
		★		F	Y	1234	Y	Y	N
		★		F	N	234	N	Y	N
			★	M	Y	234	Y	Y	Y
			★	M	N	34	Y	N	N
			★	M	N	2	N	Y	N
			★	M	N	23	Y	Y	N
			★	F	N	34	Y	Y	N
			★	F	N	234	Y	Y	Y
			★	F	N	123	Y	Y	N
			★	F	N	3	Y	Y	N
			★	F	N	23	Y	N	N

Fig. 7.7 Master sheet of responses to the survey of Humberside/South East preferences (ref. Figure 5.4)

*Always check –
'Is this relevant
to my project?'*

Using primary data

Having organized your data, you need to consider it and try to relate it to the problem which you are examining. The master sheet will now be the basis of your work. One useful approach is to take one survey question at a time. If it is a closed question, add up the number of responses in each category and compare the totals. You could compare the 'raw' numbers or convert them into percentages or fractions.

Example

Consider the master sheet shown in Figure 7.8. Look at the question 'Do you like living in Humberside?' ('Like Humb?'). There were 32 'yes' responses and 12 'no's, i.e. **73 per cent 'yes'** (32/44 × 100 per cent) and **27 per cent 'no'**. You could say that about **three quarters** of the sample like living in Humberside and a **quarter** do not.

The next step is to present the data neatly using some of the various methods of presentation described in Section Six. From then on you can treat your information in the same way as secondary data.

Using secondary source material

Secondary data comes in many forms – narrative, figures, diagrams, etc. There are several general pieces of guidance which should be kept in mind when considering data in any form:

1 The **title** and **date** of the data are most important. These give you an idea of how useful and up-to-date the data will be. Textbooks are notorious for having old statistics, whilst current editions of official sources (e.g. *Economic Trends*) are most likely to have the latest available information.

2 The **source** of the data can be a useful guide to its value. Official statistics are usually more reliable than figures put out by pressure groups. Pressure groups (including political parties) tend to be selective and may present the data in a biased way.

3 The **units of measurement** are particularly important when looking at figures (tables or graphs). Sometimes students do not notice what something is 'measured in'.

4 Watch out for **index numbers**. They are often used instead of actual amounts, particularly when talking about prices, wages and inflation. Index numbers show the **change** in a quantity (e.g. price), rather than the actual value. If the numbers are 'indexed', look for the **'base year'** to see how useful the data is – generally, the older the base year, the less useful the data.

5 Consider the **trends** shown and any **variations** from the trends. Simple comparisons can be made between **highest and lowest** figures and **oldest and newest** information.

Examples

Some of the general pieces of guidance just given are well illustrated in the example in Figure 7.8:

1 The four diagrams are all **clearly titled**, with each title summarizing the diagram's content.

2 Energy use and world oil consumption are shown by **index numbers**. The **base period** is given (an average of 1971 and 1973 figures). We are not told the actual amount of energy used or oil consumed, only how much has been used/consumed compared with 1971–73.

3 The **sources** of information used by the writer to illustrate his/her article are stated (Chevron, OECD, BP and IEA). They are reputable sources – official bodies and large companies – therefore the data is likely to be reliable.

west Germany has seen the real cost of oil fall by 15% this year, France by 14%, and Britain by 20% (see chart). A continuation of that trend could lend some support

Oil prices in real terms*
November 1987
% fall since early January

US$ C$ Lira FFr DM ¥ £   0
                                 - %
                                 5
                                 10
                                 15
                                 20

Energy use per unit of GNP
100
90   Western Europe
80   United States
70   Japan
1971-73=100
1971 75 80 85 87†

Oil prices
North Sea Brent
22 $ per barrel
20
18
16
J F M A M J J A S O N
1987

World oil consumption†
115
110
105
100 1971-73=100
1971 75 80 85 87†

* Local currency, deflated by changes in consumer prices †Estimate ‡Non-communist world
Sources: Chevron; OECD; BP; IEA

to demand in Japan and Europe even if GDP growth slows.

That may not help OPEC much. Although it has been widely advertised that

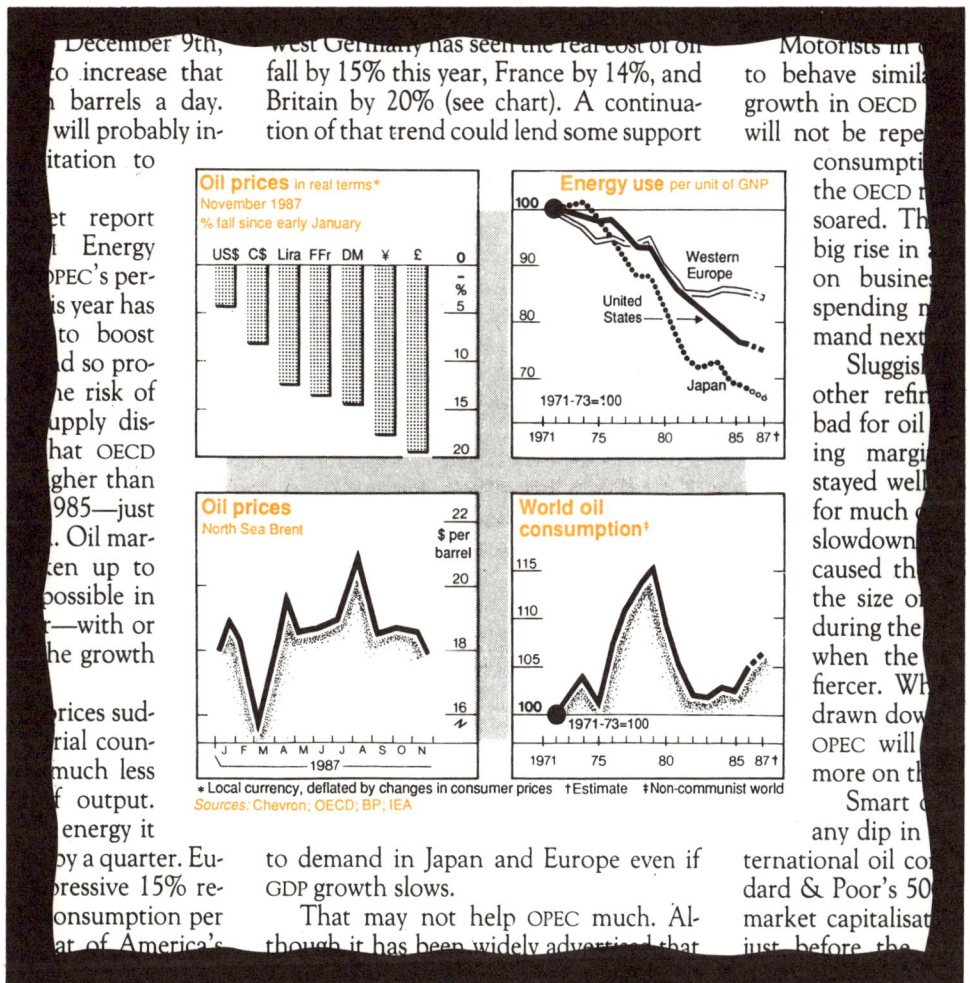

Fig. 7.8 Secondary source material – illustrations reprinted from 'A world awash with oil', *The Economist*, November 14, 1987, p.76

4 The **trends** can be quickly identified, partly because of the way the graphs have been constructed: The 'Oil prices' graph shows that world oil prices fluctuated between 15 and 21 US dollars per barrel during 1987. The average price for the period is $18, but the 'Oil prices in real term' bar chart shows that the real value actually fell in most major economies during 1987.

Calculations

We have seen **basic totalling** demonstrated in the section on handling primary data. In addition to these basic figures, the following **simple statistics** can be used to make some valuable observations about numerical data:

1 The mean: This is what is usually meant by '**the average**'. It is calculated by adding the values of all the data together, then dividing the total by the number of items. For example, the mean of 4, 7, 6, 7 and 16 is 8:

$$\frac{4 + 7 + 6 + 7 + 16}{5} = \frac{40}{5} = 8$$

2 The median: This is the value of the **middle** item, when the data are arranged in order (increasing or decreasing). In the above example, the median is 7. (The data have to be rearranged in order: 4, 6, **7**, 7, 16.)
If there are an even number of items, the median is the average of the values of the two middle item. For example, the median of 3, 4, **6, 7**, 7, and 16 is 6.5 (the average of 6 and 7).

3 The mode: This is simply the most frequently occurring value. In the above example, the mode is 7.

Example

In the following each of the calculations has been made from some actual data. All the amounts of £10 or over were treated as £10 to keep things fairly simple.

Amount earned (£ per Week)	Number of people
0	2
1	0
2	2
3	1
4	0
5	4
6	3
7	1
8	1
9	0
10+	6

Table 7.1 Summary of data from a survey of earnings from part-time work

$Mean = £6$ $\left(\dfrac{120}{20}, \text{i.e.} \dfrac{\text{total earnings}}{\text{total number of people}}\right)$

$Median = £6$
(The 20 amounts in order are 0,0,2,2,3,5,5,5,5,6,6,6,7,8,10,10,10,10,10 and 10. The median is the average of the 10th and 11th items.)

$Mode = £10+$ (This occurs most frequently – six times.)

Another useful distinction can be made between **absolute and relative change**. An **absolute change** is given in **actual numbers**, e.g. 'unemployment has decreased by half a million' (from 2½ million to 2 million). A **relative change** is expressed in **percentage terms**, e.g. 'unemployment has decreased by 20 per cent'.

The relative change is calculated by expressing the absolute change as a percentage of the original figure. In the above example, the change was from 2½ million to 2 million:

$$\textbf{relative change} = \frac{\textbf{actual change}}{\textbf{original value}} \times \textbf{100\%}$$

$$= \frac{500\,000}{2\,500\,000} \times 100\% = 20\%$$

Be careful when using relative changes. They tend to be exaggerated with small numbers, suggesting a bigger change than is actually the case.

In addition to the general guidance given so far, there are some specific points which should be noted for the following types of data:

Tables of figures

When examining tables of figures you should particularly look
- along the rows
- down the columns
- at the first and last data to see if there is an overall trend
- for similar changes in different variables

Example

The following are some valid interpretations of table 7.2. The notes in brackets after each interpretation tell you what was looked at in order to deduce the point.

1 Each of Britain's largest trade unions, except NALGO, suffered a loss of members between 1979 and 1985. (*first and last data in each row*)

2 The biggest union (the TGWU) experienced the largest actual loss (579 000 members) and the largest percentage fall (28 per cent). (*absolute and relative change*)

Table 7.2 Membership of Britain's largest trade unions, 1979–1985 (in thousands)

Union	1979	1983	1985
TGWU	2070	1633	1491
AEU	1200	1001	1001
GMB	965	940	847
NALGO	729	784	766
NUPE	712	702	673
ASTMS	471	410	385
USDAW	462	417	390

Abbreviations: TGWU, Transport and General Workers' Union; AEU, Amalgamated Engineering Union; GMB, General Municipal Boilermakers and Allied Trades Union; NALGO, National and Local Government Officers' Association; NUPE, National Union of Public Employees; ASTMS, Association of Scientific, Technical and Managerial Staffs; USDAW, Union of Shop, Distributive and Allied Workers.

3 ASTMS and USDAW have changed places in size, as ASTMS membership declined more rapidly. (*down the columns*)

4 The loss of membership has been uneven: The two largest unions suffered more between 1979 and 1983 than in the period 1983 to 1985; for the next three largest unions, the trend was the reverse. (*first and last data and down the columns*)

5 Membership of Britain's biggest trade unions decreased significantly between 1979 and 1985, but two still have more than a million members each. (*first and last data*)

6 In 1985, NALGO'S membership has increased if compared with the 1979 figure, but compared with the 1983 figure it has declined. (*rows and first and last data*)

7 Comparing only TGWU and GMB membership changes between 1983 and 1985, the TGWU had a larger absolute fall (142 000 vs. 93 000), but a smaller relative decline (8.8 vs. 9.9 per cent). (*absolute and relative change*)

Graphic material:

Diagrams must be treated with particular care because they may include any or all of the following:

- **Abbreviated titles**: Look for qualifying comments. E.g. The chart headed 'Oil prices' in Figure 7.8 is qualified by the words 'in real terms'. As shown in that example, it is possible for values to rise in money terms but fall in real terms.

- **Accompanying notes**: Sometimes footnote signs (e.g. asterisks, *, or daggers, †) are put on the diagram to indicate explanatory notes underneath the table. In Figure 7.8 there are several such notes (also see Figure 7.9, next page).

- **Estimates**: All data for future dates and some current data will be estimated. This will be indicated either by an accompanying note (e.g in Figure 7.8) or by a dotted end to the line on the graph (e.g. Figure 7.8, 'Energy use' and 'World oil consumption' graphs).

- **Manipulated scales**: In order to save space, and sometimes to stress small changes, the full range of points on a scale may not be used. E.g. In Figure 7.8, the 'Oil prices in real terms' graph uses only the range 0 to 20 per cent (not the full range of 0 to 100 per cent). Sometimes a scale is broken usually to save space (e.g. Figure 7.9, next page).

Example

Figure 7.8 showed four sets of graphic material which, between them, featured all of the above points. The next example illustrates some of the points and also shows how much can be deduced from one fairly simple graph.

Is this a Dagger which I see before me?

... or is it an asterisk?

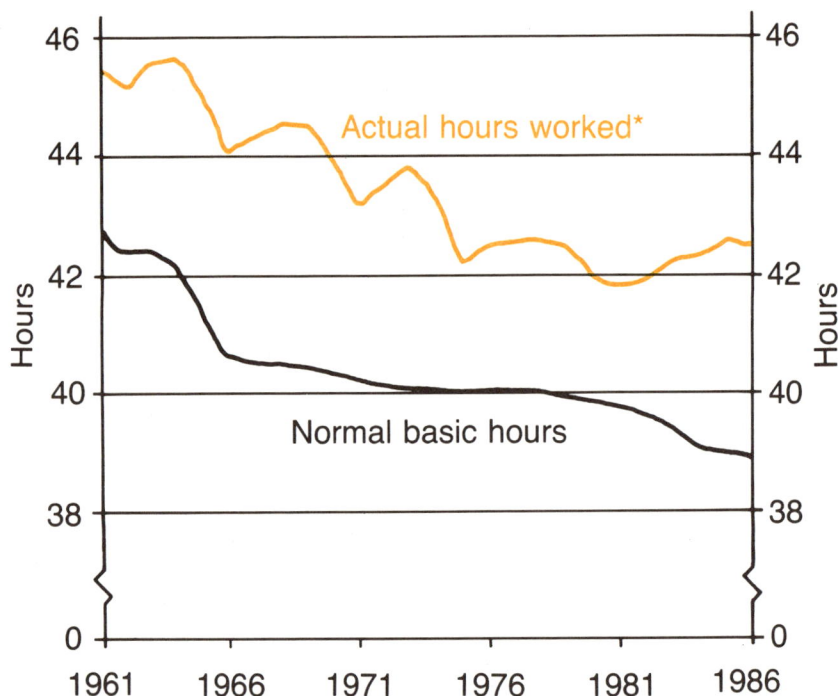

46 · · 46
44 · Actual hours worked* · 44
Hours · 42 · · 42 · Hours
40 · Normal basic hours · 40
38 · · 38
0 · · 0
1961 · 1966 · 1971 · 1976 · 1981 · 1986

*including overtime

Fig. 7.9 Average weekly hours of work in the UK, 1961–86
(*Source*: *Social Trends*, 1988)

Interpretations

(Again the notes in brackets indicate how the deductions were made.)

1 Actual hours worked has fallen in the last 25 years. (*trend*)

2 In 1961, actual hours worked were 45.4, but in 1986 they had fallen to 42.6. (*oldest and newest*)

3 Actual hours worked fell from a high of 45.7 hours in 1964 to a low of 42 hours in 1982 and 1983. (*highest and lowest*)

4 Actual hours worked did not fall smoothly. In some years they actually increased (e.g. 1966–69). (*deviations from the trend*)

Note that if you suggest a possible reason for the deviations, this would be analysis rather than simple interpretation.

5 Normal basic hours of work have fallen in last 25 years. (*trend*)

6 Normal basic hours in 1961 were 43 hours, but in 1986 they were only 38 hours. (*oldest and newest, highest and lowest*)

7 The normal basic working week fell by 5 hours between 1961 and 1986. (*calculation – simple maths*)

8 Normal basic hours fell most between 1961 and 1966 and rather slowly, but steadily, thereafter. (*deviations from trend*)

9 The difference between normal basic hours and actual hours worked is explained by overtime. (*accompanying notes*)

10 The amount of overtime worked has varied over the years. (*difference between the curves*)

11 The most overtime worked was in 1966 (4½ hours per week) and the least was 2 hours per week in 1982. (*difference between curves and calculation*)

12 The amount of overtime worked seems to be increasing since 1981. (*difference between curves and calculation*)

Here the specific points have been separately and laboriously made in separate sentences. In practice, you would probably amalgamate some to form slightly more complicated sentences on the same theme. For instance, points 1 and 4 fit well together, similarly points 5 and 8.

Interpret your data – but note its limitations!

Action for secondary data

1 Consider **title**, **date and source** of data.

2 Examine the **units** and **scale** of measurement.

3 Try to spot **trends** and **deviations** from trends in the data.

4 Distinguish between **absolute** and **relative** changes.

5 Make any appropriate **calculations**.

6 For tables of figures look along **rows**, down **columns**, at **different variables** and at **first and last** data.

7 For graphs be careful to check the scales and look for accompanying **notes** and **estimates**.

✓ Checklist

Primary data

DO ● use a master sheet
  ● devise simple codes for responses
  ● take care when categorizing responses
  ● consider questions singly
  ● compare relevant questions

Secondary data

DO ● examine title, date and source of data
  ● look at the units and scale of measurement
  ● search for trends and deviations
  ● make some calculations

DON'T ● mix up absolute and relative changes

Analysis

To analyse something is to think about it in detail and make **deductions**. In Economics coursework you will be analysing an economic problem. Your deductions are comments which try to give an insight into the problem.

Application involved ideas/data and a problem – you started with concepts and decided whether or not they were relevant to your problem. Analysis also involves principles and a problem, but the thought process is reversed: you **start with the problem** (or some data) and search for any principles or ideas which might explain the situation (or data). In practice, you make deductions from your findings in order to answer the question or discuss the problem which is the title of your coursework assignment. You may have had some ideas (possible answers) at the back of your mind, or on paper, at the beginning of the exercise. You will need to decide which of your ideas have been revealed in the data which you have collected.

Analysis takes place after the data has been collected, presented and interpreted. Interpretation is the description of what the data shows; analysis goes a step further. Interpretation describes **what** occurred; analysis attempts to explain **why** things occur. In practice, it is very difficult to divorce interpretation from analysis. A summary of the main points in your analysis section will form your 'Conclusion'.

Factors in successful analysis

When you solve problems with reasoned answers you are analysing. It is useful to understand something of how you do this – what is happening in your mind. Much research in psychology has been devoted to explaining the problem-solving process. Psychologists have identified six general factors or characteristics common to people who are successful analysts:

1 Memory	4 General intelligence
2 Knowledge	5 Content-related experience
3 Motivation	6 A planned approach

Let us consider each of these factors in turn:

1 Memory

There is not a lot that this book can do to improve your memory, but it is possible to train your memory. Your school may run courses in study skills in which memory training is often a component. Remembering strategies (how to do things) is as important as remembering facts.

2 Knowledge

Your **classroom learning** in Economics is clearly important for your coursework. You should not consider your coursework completely separate from normal classroom work.

If you choose an assignment which does not link up with your current work in class, you will need to refresh your memory about your chosen theme by referring to your notebook and textbook as discussed in Section Five. It is no coincidence that those who generally work hard and accumulate knowledge (including **'general knowledge'**) produce the best coursework.

3 Motivation

Motivation comes with **being interested** in what you are doing. This makes analysis easier because you want to 'find something out'. Hence the earlier advice to choose a title or subject in which you are interested.

4 General intelligence

I cannot help there, but don't underestimate yourself.

5 Content-related experience

This phrase means having considered similar problems before or having experience directly related to the problem under consideration. If you have chosen a topic related to your part-time job or hobby you will have considerable content-related experience. You may also be familiar with the assignment requirements from having done a practice assignment. If your teacher does not set you a practice assignment, the model assignment in Appendix 2 should be useful.

6 A planned approach

If you approach your analysis systematically you are more likely to achieve success than if you search randomly for possible solutions. If you follow the advice given in this book, you should be quite well organized.

The effectiveness of the analysis used to solve problems is determined by:

(a) How you process information – the sections on the collection and presentation of data give you a framework.

(b) The structure of the problem – our approach has been to develop subsidiary questions (e.g. the individual questions in your survey questionnaire) which help to answer the central problem or 'prove' the main hypothesis.

(c) The strategies you use – when analysing data, the 'strategies' are the questions which you need to ask about each piece of information. The following list of questions assumes that you have decided that the information is relevant to your problem and that you have interpreted the data as explained in pages 58–63.

Data analysis – questions to ask

The first seven questions can be applied to most pieces of data. Questions 8 to 10 require comparisons between two or more pieces of data.

1 Can I think of **a reason** for this result/data (trend, deviation, etc)?

2 Can I think of **other possible explanations** for this result/data?

3 Which of the possible reasons is **most likely** and **why**?

4 Are there **any economic concepts** which my results/data illustrate?

5 Are there **any other economic concepts** which may be relevant?

6 Does the evidence or knowledge gathered support a particular **point of view**?

7 Is the **source** of the data **reliable or biased**?

8 Are there **other pieces of data** which lead to the **same answer/conclusion** (which illustrate the same principles)?

9 Are there **other pieces of data** which suggest **different answers/ conclusions** (and thus illustrate different, possibly conflicting, principles)?

10 What might **explain** the possible difference(s)?

Analysis may be undertaken at different times as you proceed with your assignment. You might initially analyse some existing secondary material in order to prepare some general remarks for your Introduction. However, most analysis will be done after you have carried out some investigation of your own. As well as a section called 'Analysis', a summary of your main findings should also appear in your 'Conclusion'.

Examples

Analysis of secondary data

1 **Assignment title – 'Privatization has gone too far.'**

£10m council care crisis spurs privatisation plan

By A Correspondent

Privatisation of large sections of a county council's social services department is being considered after a warning the authority will need £10 million more for community care over the next 10 years.

Hereford and Worcester county council has set up a special working party to find a more economical method of running old peoples' homes, children's homes and services for the mentally and physically handicapped.

The working party, which is expected to present a report in January, is concerned about an anticipated increase in the county's pensioner population over the next 30 years.

The leader of the Conservative-controlled council, Mr David Finch, said privatisation was one option being considered to tackle the substantial increase in social services spending.

"My own view is that every area should be examined for privatisation, but it is also my philosophy that no people who need a service should receive a worse service, or be affected in any way," he said.

"Any civilised society must look after its old and disadvantaged residents, but there are various ways of looking after them. There is going to be a distinct change over the next decade."

The the National and Local Government Officers Association said it was planning to join with the Confederation of Health Service Employees and the National Union of Public Employees to resist any attempt to privatise the services.

"Over the past three years there have been horrendous cases of ill-treatment in privately-run old people's homes, and most ordinary people will feel safer opting for life in a local authority home," said Mr Paul Griffiths, the Nalgo county secretary.

Fig. 7.10 Reprinted from *The Guardian*, 16 November 1987

Several of the ten questions given above to aid analysis are not relevant to this **narrative data**. However, those which are relevant lead to the following valid comments:

Qn 1 – Privatisation is a topical subject.

Qn 5 – Increase in pensioner population.

– Desire for efficiency in running old people's homes, etc.

Qn 6 – County Council view, i.e. the need to tackle increases in social services spending.

– Trade union view, i.e. resist privatization because local authority homes are safer.

There could be underlying motives for both these views. It is a Conservative ideal to reduce the role of the public sector, hence the Conservative-dominated council may be using the need to stop spending increases as a means of divesting the council of social service responsibilities. The trade unions may fear that job losses and/or pay cuts for their members would follow privatization; this could be why they seek to maintain the present arrangements.

Qn 7 – The source can be treated as reliable. It is a reputable newspaper. The article has an objective heading, reports the facts and both points of view have been presented.

2 Extract from a talk by A. Mitchell MP (Labour) to the Economics Association, Humberside Branch, March 1987.

> I believe that natural monopolies are better regulated in public ownership, than in the private sector. Thus I oppose privatization . . . Furthermore, the sale of assets has been irresponsible. Brokers have fleeced civil servants, there have been expensive advertising campaigns (remember 'Tell Sid') and assets have been deliberately underpriced . . . I calculate that one and a half billion has been lost on seven privatizations.
>
> What about the Government's arguments? They argue that wider share ownership has been achieved. However, the bulk of the shares have gone to the institutions; many small shareholders sold off their shares quickly. It has not taught the virtues of investment, just the benefits of speculation. It is a 'casino mentality' . . .

Again, several of our ten analytical questions are not relevant, but the following comments can be made:

Qn 1 – Privatization is a major political issue.

Qn 5 – Natural monopoly, underpriced assets, wider share ownership, investment, speculation.

Qn 6 – Yes, anti-privatization.

Qn 7 – Probably biased, (politically).

Qns 8 & 9 – The talk is more emotive than the newspaper article. It is more general and wide-ranging in its approach.

Q 10 – An attempt to convert an audience and/or to put a viewpoint different to that of another speaker.

Analysis of primary data

3 Case study of a travel agency

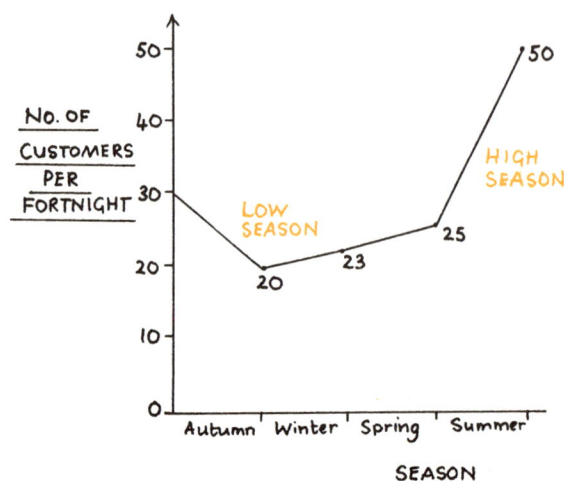

Fig. 7.11 Travel agency bookings by season

The student who did this case study analysed the reasons for the variation in ticket bookings:

> During the last month of the Islamic year muslims from all over the world go on a pilgrimage to Mecca and Medina (in Saudi Arabia). To reach Saudi Arabia you obviously need a ticket, therefore our community, being an Asian one, buys their tickets from an Asian travel agent. As the agent is a muslim, the customers rely on him. He has been on the pilgrimage himself so he can give them a lot of advice. At this time of year there are many discounts, especially on this HAJ, or pilgrim service.

He used our first two questions in his analysis but he could have gone further. He could also have used the following questions:

Qn 3 – He might have directly stated which he thought was the main reason, rather than implying it.

Qn 4 – He could have related his reasons to economic ideas and concepts, such as specialization (catering for Asian pilgrimages), non-price advantage/competition (trust of the agent), seasonal fluctuations in demand (as shown in graph), elasticity of demand (price discounts).

Qn 5 – He could have brought in other relevant economics ideas not directly illustrated, for example the nature of the competition. A competitor, Thomas Cook, was mentioned elsewhere in the case study but the two agencies were not compared.

Qns 8–10 – If he had obtained information from Thomas Cook or collected some general data on holidays, comparative analysis might have been possible. However, because the assignment was principally a case study, questions 8–10 are less significant than if the student had been hypothesis testing.

4 Assignment title – 'Is the advertising of cigarettes and cigars efficient?'

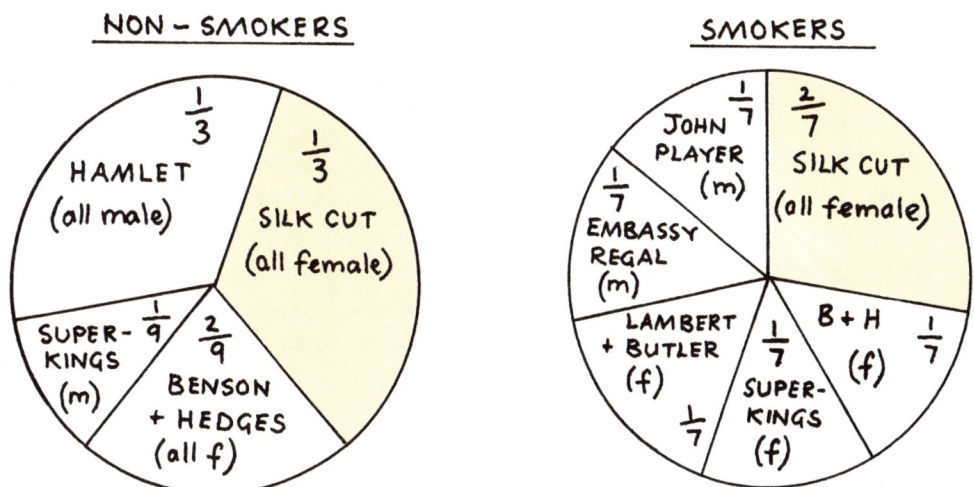

NON – SMOKERS

SMOKERS

Fig. 7.12 Favourite cigar/cigarette advertisements

In this assignment, the student not only answered the central question but also discovered something else about such advertising. This arose from the subsidiary questions which she asked in her survey. The question 'What is your favourite cigar/cigarette advertisement?' produced the data illustrated in Figure 7.12 (previous page).

Her 'Interpretation' section included the following comment:

> 'Among the non-smokers, the females liked Silk Cut and Benson and Hedges advertisements, while the males preferred advertisements for Hamlet and Superkings. . . . Even among the smokers, Silk Cut adverts were exclusively liked by women.'

In the 'Analysis', she gave possible reasons:

> 'Men seem to prefer humorous ones such as the Hamlet cigar advertisements. Women prefer those which use the name of the cigarettes in an unusual way, e.g. the Silk Cut advertisement.'

This example partly illustrates the use of our questions 8 to 10.

✓ Checklist – Analysis

DO
- think of reasons why
- consider alternative explanations
- apply concepts and ideas
- compare data from different sources (or survey questions)
- try to explain differences

DON'T
- just describe the data
- assume opinions/sources are unbiased
- ignore conflicting results

Making judgments

There are many aspects to the skill of evaluation or judgment making. Most of your judgments will appear in your 'Conclusion', but there will be opportunities to demonstrate your evaluation skills in other parts of the assignment for example in the 'Methods' section. In your 'Conclusion', you should make judgments over two broad areas: Firstly evaluate **what** you have discovered – your findings; then judge **how** you discovered it – your methods. You will need to re-read your 'Introduction', 'Investigation', 'Analysis' and 'Methods' sections.

Conclusions on findings

Begin with the obvious. Give **a direct answer** to the main question in your title. If you have developed several supplementary questions which lead up to the main question, deal with them first then draw a general conclusion.

Give **reasons** for your judgments. These should have been generated during interpretation and analysis of the data. In the 'Conclusion' you should extract the main points from these earlier sections. Try not to write out the same thing again, but really **emphasize the main point(s)**.

Your results should always be treated with **great caution**. The earlier remarks about unrepresentative samples (in Section Five, page 21) must be kept in mind. The following are useful **qualifying words and phrases**:

might	(instead of 'will');
could	(instead of 'is');
may	(instead of 'must');
seems to	(instead of 'does').

Adjectives such as 'perhaps', 'maybe' and 'probably' can also be used to show the reader of your assignment that you recognize the limitations of your work.

When your assignment includes the views and opinions of different people you must consider them critically. Try to **distinguish between fact and opinion**. For instance, the statement that 'Firm A sells more products than Firm B' is a fact, whereas the statement that 'Firm A sells better products than Firm B' is a matter of opinion. As a student of Economics you need to show that you can make such distinctions. If you use information from an 'expert' and you feel he/she is biased, do not be afraid to say so, but give reasons.

Unusual or unexpected findings need to be given weight in your 'Conclusion'. If you were led to expect one thing by your preliminary reading or economic theory and you discover something different, do not be afraid to say so. Again, give reasons or possible reasons for the difference.

Example

A student investigating the costs and benefits of Sunday trading wrote:

> 'According to many secondary sources prices will fall. I found that the shops I asked would not reduce prices. One store said they would have to increase prices to cover the increased staff costs.'

In your conclusion you could also **speculate** about possible future research in the area you have considered. You could suggest follow-up activities and/or maybe survey questionnaires.

A different type of conclusion is sometimes needed if you have operated a **mini-enterprise**. The written report may only be part of the assessment. Practical activities and group discussions may also be observed and assessed. If the mini-enterprise was operated by a group, each student will have to report not only on the enterprise but also on their own contribution.

Example

One member of a group who organized a cafe selling sandwiches, cakes and hot drinks wrote the following:

> 'I learnt that if we want to keep trade the most important aspect of the business was to ensure that our customers were pleased with our products and our service. If there was a complaint, then it was our duty to refund the customer's money or give them another sample of goods. . . .
>
> General attitudes toward the company, its workers and its progress were also very important. One of the personnel was demoted for lack of responsibility and a 'slap happy', 'can't be bothered' attitude. This kind of behaviour, we decided, did not make a good working atmosphere.'

As well as these perspective comments, she also pointed out mistakes and suggested ways of improving the enterprise:

> 'Our stock, for instance, was in a shambles, with no regular check kept. In future, I would suggest that one person's role would be to make very regular stock checks and keep the books in order.
>
> Another improvement which I would make would be on the advertising side of the business. The posters that were issued were not very informative. In future, I would like to see much brighter and more interesting advertisements.
>
> Also, a regular weekly meeting with all the recent problems and discussion points raised could help to clear the air and let everyone know what is going on.'

It is sometimes possible to make **general comments** in your conclusions which could apply to other problems or other businesses. You may feel that what you have discovered may be relevant to other pieces of research.

Example

A student examining the new car market argued that the advertisers should distinguish between potential customers and people 'just browsing'. He argued:

'. . . people just browsing are not the target of the advertising but unfortunately for the car companies they make up the majority of the readers/viewers. Obviously most people seeing a car advertisement on television will not be the faintest bit interested in buying a car, but a potential customer may be watching. It is a form of gambling.'

Conclusions on methods

You will need to appraise your research methods **objectively** and **critically**. The first step is to comment on your general approach. Mention any **problems** which arose, how you dealt with them and possible effects on the quality of your findings. Any **mistakes** which you made should be frankly admitted – for example, not leaving sufficient time to question the full quota in one of the stratified groups of your sample.

Having considered the problems and mistakes you are then in a position to consider the **limitations** of the method(s) used. Be brutally honest! If you only collected 23 opinions, making data presentation, interpretation and analysis difficult, say so. This enables you to explain how a similar assignment should be planned and conducted in future. Such thoughtful comments will probably earn extra marks.

Example

In commenting on her methods, one student wrote:

> 'I interviewed people of different ages to try and get an accurate cross-section, although, realistically, my survey wasn't very accurate because I only took 24 people's opinions in a very small area of the country. If this survey was done again, I would try to ask more people, in a wider area and a greater range of ages. . . . therefore my results could vary greatly from the general view in Britain.'

Notice that this student has identified the **weaknesses** of her method and suggested future **improvements**. She has also treated her results with **caution**.

✓ Checklist

DO ● directly answer main question(s)
   ● give reasons
   ● treat your findings with caution
   ● criticize your work
   ● comment on methods
   ● make suggestions for improvements and future research

DON'T ● be too categorical
   ● dismiss unusual discoveries
   ● copy out earlier work – summarize!

SECTION EIGHT

Finishing touches

Until now we have looked at specific aspects of the coursework assignment, e.g. planning, surveys, etc., in isolation. The parts must be combined to form a whole – your completed assignment. A general format was outlined in Section Three (page 10). Table 8.1 shows where each major section of the assignment is significantly featured in this book. You can use the table to check that you have covered everything.

Table 8.1 Where the major assignment sections are featured in this book

Assignment section	Relevant section in this book
Introduction	3 Forward planning 4 Titles 7 Application and analysis of data
Investigation	3 Forward planning 5 Collection of data 6 Presentation of data 7 Application and analysis of data
Analysis	3 Forward planning 6 Presentation of data 7 Application and analysis of data
Methods	3 Forward planning 5 Collection of data 6 Presentation of data 7 Application and analysis of data
Conclusion	3 Forward planning 7 Application and analysis of data

If you refer back to the standard format, you will see that there are **three other sections** to be added to complete the assignment: the '**List of contents**', the '**Bibliography**' and the '**Appendices**'. I will look at them in the order in which they should be prepared.

The bibliography

As explained in Section Three, this section should include a list of the books, journal articles, magazines, newspapers, etc., which you have used. They should be listed in **alphabetical order** according to the name of the author (for books or articles) or the name of the publication (for magazines and newspapers). Each item should begin on a new line. Each reference should begin with the **author's name** (surname, then initials), followed by the **title**, **publisher** and the **year of publication**.

Example

Leake, A., '*Action Economics*' (Macmillan Education Ltd, 1986)

West, K. C., '*Revise Economics*' (Charles Letts & Co Ltd, 1985)

Appendices

This section was described in Section Three and is also mentioned in Section Five ('Collection of data'). It should include such things as:

—complete copies of **cuttings** from which information was taken
—copies of **letters** to, and replies from , 'experts'
—examples of completed **survey sheets**
—rough **drafts** of material
—**raw data**
—survey **master sheet**
—a list of **people who helped** you

The exhibits should be numbered so that they can easily be referred to in the main text of your assignment. Ideally, they should be in the same order as they appear in the text.

The list of contents

This is the last piece in the jigsaw. The list of contents is simply a list of the chapter (section) headings, together with the number of the page on which each chapter starts. You will need to number all of the pages of writing (and diagrams if they take up a whole page) before preparing your list of contents. The list should be inserted after the title page and before the 'Introduction'.

Example

APPENDIX 1

Syllabus analysis

Syllabus	SEG	NEA (A)	NEA (B)	LEAG	MEG	NISEC	WJEC
Knowledge and understanding / information gathering	3	11¼	5	5	9.3	4	6
Presentation	4	11¼	5	5	9.3	4	6
Application	6½	11¼	5	10	15.7	6	6
Analysis	6½	11¼	5	10	15.7	4	6
Evaluation (judgment)	6½	7½	5	5		4	8
Total coursework %	20	30	20	25	25	20	20
Raw marks per assignment	25	40	16	33	40	20	20
Numbers of assignments	2	1–3	3	3	3	1	2
Word length	750–1000	3×1000 or 2×1500 or 1×1000	500–750	1000	1000	2000	1000–2000

Examination groups: addresses

London   University of London Schools Examinations Board
                  Stewart House, 32 Russell Square, London WC1B 5DN

LREB   London Regional Examinations Board
                  Lyon House, 104 Wandsworth High Street, London SW18 4LF

EAEB   East Anglian Examinations Board
                  The Lindens, Lexden Road, Colchester, Essex CO3 3RL (0206 549595)

Cambridge   University of Cambridge Local Examinations Syndicate
                  Syndicate Buildings, 1 Hills Road, Cambridge CB1 2EU (0223 61111)

O & C   Oxford and Cambridge Schools Examinations Board
                  10 Trumpington Street, Cambridge CB2 1QB and Elsfield Way, Oxford
                  OX2 8EP

SUJB   Southern Universities' Joint Board for School Examinations
                  Cotham Road, Bristol BS6 6DD

WMEB   West Midlands Examinations Board
                  Norfolk House, Smallbrook Queensway, Birmingham B5 4NJ

EMREB   East Midland Regional Examinations Board
                  Robins Wood House, Robins Wood Road, Aspley, Nottingham NG8 3NR

                                          (write to your local board.)
JMB   Joint Matriculation Board (061-273 2565)
                  Devas Street, Manchester M15 6EU *(also for centres outside the NEA area)*

ALSEB   Associated Lancashire Schools Examining Board
                  12 Harter Street, Manchester M1 6HL

NREB   North Regional Examinations Board
                  Wheatfield Road, Westerhope, Newcastle upon Tyne NE5 5JZ

NWREB   North-West Regional Examinations Board
                  Orbit House, Albert Street, Eccles, Manchester M30 0WL

YHREB   Yorkshire and Humberside Regional Examinations Board
                  Harrogate Office — 31–33 Springfield Avenue, Harrogate HG1 2HW
                  Sheffield Office — Scarsdale House, 136 Derbyshire Lane, Sheffield S8 8SE

NISEC   Northern Ireland Schools Examinations Council
                  Beechill House, 42 Beechill Road, Belfast BT8 4RS (0232 704666)

SEB   Scottish Examinations Board
                  Ironmills Road, Dalkeith, Midlothian EH22 1BR (031-663 6601)

AEB   The Associated Examining Board
                  Stag Hill House, Guildford, Surrey GU2 5XJ (0483 503123)

Oxford   Oxford Delegacy of Local Examinations
                  Ewert Place, Summertown, Oxford OX2 7BZ

SREB   Southern Regional Examinations Board
                  Eastleigh House, Market Street, Eastleigh, Hampshire SO5 4SW

SEREB   South-East Regional Examinations Board
                  Beloe House, 2–10 Mount Ephraim Road, Tunbridge Wells TN1 1EU

SWEB   South-Western Examinations Board
                  23–29 Marsh Street, Bristol BS1 4BP

WJEC   Welsh Joint Education Committee
                  245 Western Avenue, Cardiff CF5 2YX (0222 561231)

(The boards to which you should write are underlined in each case.)

APPENDIX 2

A model assignment

The following assignment has been included to illustrate many of the points made in this book. It is based on an actual assignment submitted for GCSE Economics. The candidate was not a student of the author and the assignment has been modified slightly so that it conforms to the structure which he has recommended. The work was actually carried out and the data are unaltered. The 'Analysis' and 'Conclusions' have also been left largely untouched. A brief introduction and a 'Methods' section have been added; the 'Methods' section is based on the candidate's footnote to her original conclusion.

G.C.S.E Economics Coursework

Juliet Wells

HYPOTHESIS :-

Price is the most important factor when people choose a hairdresser.

IMFORMATION SOURCES : -

A survey compiled by myself and completed by members of the public in Grimsby.

LIST OF CONTENTS

INTRODUCTION

This assignment is concerned with the factors that influence people's choice of hairdresser. A hair-do is a service. It was a luxury in the past but it is less so today. This is because of the improvements in living standards in Britain, which have enabled women to visit the hairdressers more frequently.

Many women are now wage earners and so have more control over their spending. They tend to use hairdressers more than men do.

The factors which I shall consider are demand factors. According to economic theory, demand is effective when backed by money. Individual demand is determined by either price or the conditions of demand. In theory, for a normal good, at a high price there is low demand. On the other hand at a low price there is high demand. The conditions of demand include any other non-price factor e.g. the reputation of a hairdressing salon. If the conditions of demand for a hairdresser become more favourable, there will be an increase in the demand for their service. Conversely, if the conditions become less favourable then demand will fall.

The survey was carried out at two hairdressers and at school. This gave a good mix of young and old, male and female. The two hairdressers were different in style too: one was the biggest in town, the other a small partnership.

INVESTIGATION

HYPOTHESIS: - Price is the most important factor
when people choose a hairdresser.

To try to prove this hypothesis a survey was
constructed, consisting of ten demand factors. Members
of the public were asked to decide whether they thought
each of the factors was very important (3), important
(2) or not important at all (1), when choosing a hairdresser.
The ten factors were : -
Price of treatment
Location of salon
Reputation of salon
Staff treatment
Opening hours
Atmosphere of salon
Quality of treatment
External appearance of salon
Internal appearance of salon
Range of treatments

Whilst completing the survey the public came up
with three more factors :-
Waiting time (3 points = very important that you DON'T
have to wait long for treatment).
Compliance by staff to do what's requested.
Cleanliness of salon.

I eventually interviewed 40 people — 18 at
'Inn Trim', 10 at the partnership and 12 at school.
The answers given to my questions by each
respondent are included in the Appendix.

RESULTS

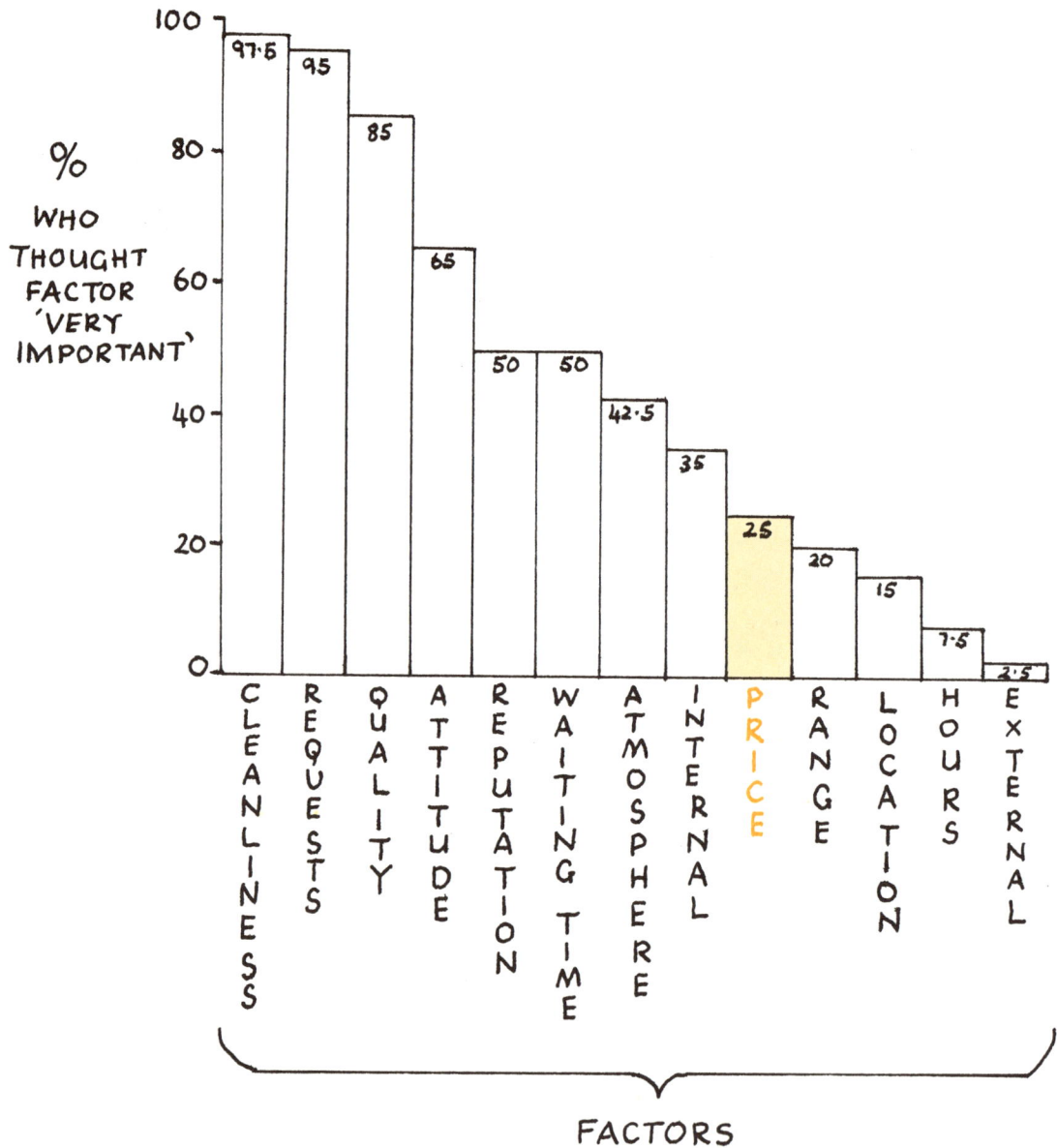

% WHO THOUGHT FACTOR 'VERY IMPORTANT'

Bar chart values from left to right:
- CLEANLINESS: 97.5
- REQUESTS: 95
- QUALITY: 85
- ATTITUDE: 65
- REPUTATION: 50
- WAITING TIME: 50
- ATMOSPHERE: 42.5
- INTERNAL: 35
- PRICE: 25
- RANGE: 20
- LOCATION: 15
- HOURS: 7.5
- EXTERNAL: 2.5

FACTORS

Figure 1 :   Importance of various factors

(Importance was calculated by dividing number of
3's by 40, that is the number surveyed, and
multiplying by 100 to get a percentage,
e.g. cleanliness $\frac{39}{40} \times 100 = 97.5\%$)

Juliet Wells

Taking into account the whole survey one discovers PRICE isn't the most important demand factor for a hairdresser: the cleanliness of the place came top, followed closely by 'Obedience to requests' (that is, the stylist does what you ask).

Looking at the results you see that 'price' comes near to the bottom in importance; only 25% of the people questioned in the survey thought price was very important. Compared to the 97.5% who thought cleanliness very important, it isn't a lot. Suprisingly, 'quality of treatment' came third in importance with 85% of the survey thinking it was very important. (Considering that the only reason for going to the hairdressers is to have some sort of treatment, one would've thought everyone would want a good quality job done.) There were even two people who thought 'quality of treatment' not important at all.

The range of treatments performed by the salon makes very little difference to the average customer. In the survey it came tenth out of thirteen factors. Even less important were location, opening hours and external appearances. It seems reasonable to suppose that a clean hair salon will have more business than one which performs lots of different treatments, but isn't clean. Therefore, the opportunity cost of paying a highly skilled hairdresser is to pay a cleaner and at the same time increase business.

Table 1 :

<u>Importance of factors at each hairdresser</u>

FACTOR	MAIN SALON	PARTNERSHIP
Cleanliness	1	2
Obedience to requests	1	4
Quality of treatment	4	1
Staff attitude	3	2
Atmosphere	8	5
Waiting time	7	5
Reputation	6	7
Internal appearance	5	9
PRICE	9	8
Range of treatments	10	11
Location	11	10
Opening hours	13	13
External appearance	12	12

Table 1 backs up the theory that price isn't really important. One major difference between the salon and the partnership is that in the partnership the quality of treatment is three places higher and is the most important factor for the people who go there. Obviously the treatment there must be very good - so good in fact that cleanliness and external appearance don't matter so much. The survey results suggest that the majority of people who went to the main salon in town go there because of its cleanliness and staff.

One factor both groups agree is not important is the hairdresser's opening hours. It comes last in importance for both salons. The location isn't so important and this suggests people are prepared to travel if treatment is good and the place is clean. Location may not be so important for the salon in the town because a lot of people will come into the town on a Saturday to do some shopping and have a hair-cut at the same time.

ANALYSIS

Demand for hairdressers is relatively _inelastic_. This means that a price change will have little effect on the quantity demanded (fig. 2).

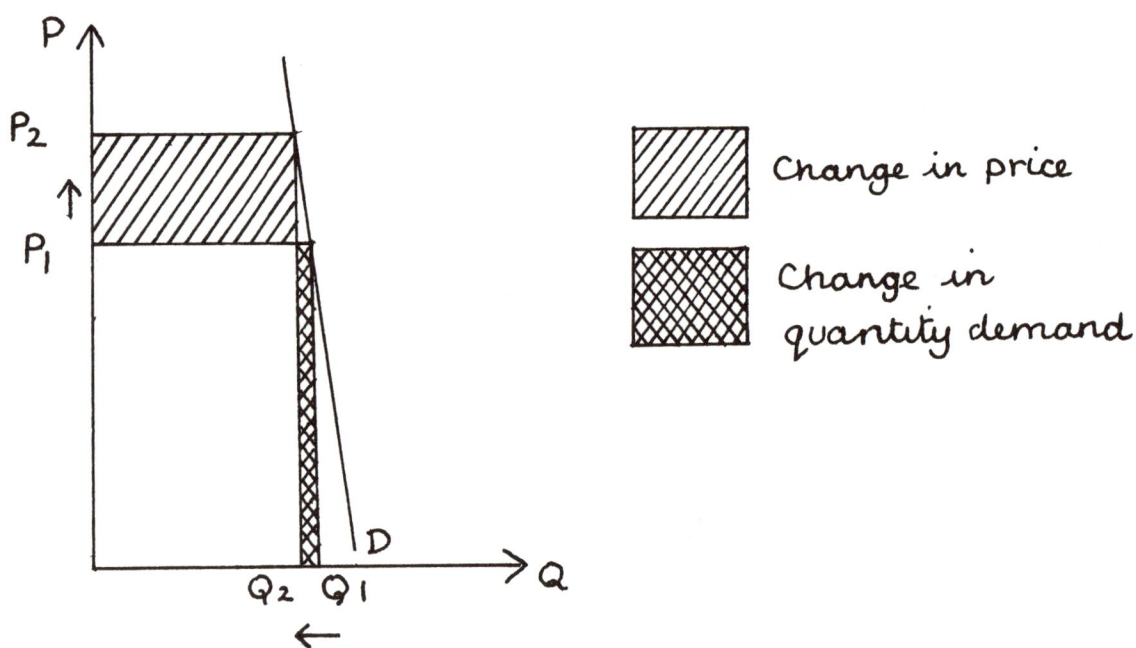

Figure 2: Inelastic demand

The following are possible reasons why the demand is inelastic:

(a) There is only one substitute for having your hair cut and that is growing it long. Unfortunately, many people do not like this alternative, especially men, and even long hair still needs regular trimming to keep it in a good condition.

(b) The proportion of income spent on a trip to the hairdresser is relatively small compared with, say, that of the cost of a car.

Juliet Wells

(c) Many people think haircuts are essential so however high prices go there'll always be customers.

The majority of people go to the hairdresser to satisfy their vanity. They want to look good and so put quality of treatment before price. (see figure 1 or table 1). This gives hairdressers power over their price lists. As shown by the survey, people aren't really bothered by the price of treatment so long as it is good, the place is clean, and the staff treat you well and comply with your requests.

Prices are also kept high by a limitation of hairdressers. You need to be specially trained and skilled to practise hairdressing commercially. This means the majority of people have to rely on the minority of who have specialized in this particular field (an example of 'division of labour') and pay what they want to charge. The demand for hairdressing is forever present partly because fashions change and therefore hairstyles change.

There is a limit to how much a stylist can charge and if his prices are very high his customers will go elsewhere. But, hairdressers can afford to raise prices fairly high because as explained earlier, the demand is inelastic.

For example: A hairdresser raised his price for a cut and blow-dry from £6 to £10. Some customers wouldn't be prepared to pay this and so take their custom elsewhere. This is a decrease in supply (fig. 3). Even so, the hairdresser would be making a greater revenue.

Juliet Wells

Figure 3:
Effect of price rise on the demand for a cut and blow-dry.

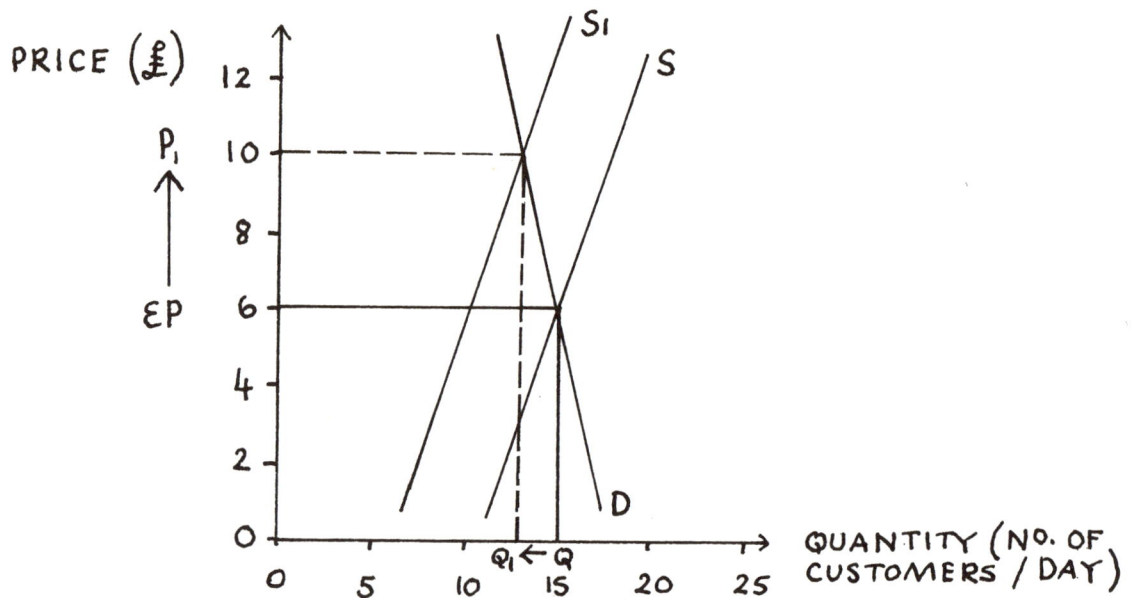

total revenue = price × quantity demanded.
　"　　　"　　when a cut costs £6 = 6 × 15 = £90
　"　　"　　　"　　"　　"　　"　　£10 = 10 × 13 = £130

Even though there were fewer customers, the increase in price made up for the loss.

From the survey results one wouldn't class price as a factor hairdressers would compete for custom with. Of course this would vary, depending on a customer's financial situation e.g. an unemployed person wouldn't spend £10 on a haircut when down the road a cut costs £3. It may not include a blow dry but it serves the same purpose and costs a lot less money, which is a scarce resource for an unemployed person.
In hairdressing there doesn't seem to be an outstanding factor on which to compete but

Juliet Wells

several. The competition between salons lies in
  cleanliness,
  staff,
  quality of treatment,
  obedience of requests,
  and promptness.

Therefore they are the most important factors - the
factors competing hairdressers will try to improve to
increase business.

As everyone needs some sort of hair treatment, whether
it be a cut, a perm or whatever, there are many customers
for salons to compete for. Customers are needed because
competitive industries are constantly fighting for survival
and must make at least normal profits. Competition
between hairdressers is therefore very important.

Once a salon gets a customer, it wants to make sure
that it keeps that person's custom: There is no other way
except by providing a good standard of service
(i.e. maintaining a good standard in competition factors).
Many people stay with one hairdresser for years (as was
evident whilst conducting the survey). This customer
loyalty is very good because it provides an almost -
guaranteed revenue. It can also cause problems: There
could be a tendency for standards to fall if the
owner/manager becomes too complacent. If he takes
it for granted that the customers will keep coming
back, he may inadvertently let appearances and
standards slip. Once these standards start to fall
the consumer will notice and take his/her
custom elsewhere, to a competitor. So customer
loyalty is a good thing if treated properly.

METHODS

The results in this survey may be inaccurate because only a small number of people were asked their opinion. In addition the survey was unrepresentative and unbalanced. It did not include equal numbers by sex or age. A future survey to test my hypothesis should have a larger and properly stratified sample. I should have probably also looked at opinions over a period of time and covered more hairdressers in my survey.

When doing my analysis and interpretation I made some errors. Firstly I did not properly consider the people whom I surveyed at school. Their views might have contrasted with those of the adults which I interviewed in the salons. Secondly, my scoring system (ie. 3 for very important) was very simple and I did not make much use of the totals. I did not really look closely enough at differences between the two types of hairdressing establishment.

Juliet Wells

CONCLUSION

Price of treatment does not determine the hairdresser a person goes to in Grimsby. In areas of high unemployment this may vary. There are several other factors which influence the decision of which hairdresser to go to: cleanliness of salon; obedience to requests; quality of treatment; and staff attitude / treatment. These four factors are the most important and become the most competitive areas of hairdressing. Hair salons compete for customers. The loyal customer is best as he/she provides an almost guaranteed revenue.

APPENDIX

DEMAND AT A HAIRDRESSERS

JULIET WELLS

DEMAND FACTORS	SCHOOL													PARTNERSHIP									PART. TOT.
	1	2	3	4	5	6	7	8	9	10	11	12	13	14	15	16	17	18	19	20	21	22	
PRICE	2	3	2	2	3	2	2	2	2	2	2	2	1	2	3	3	1	2	3	3	2	1	21
LOCATION	2	2	1	2	2	1	1	1	2	2	2	2	1	3	2	2	2	2	3	1	1	2	18
REPUTATION	1	2	3	3	2	3	3	2	3	3	3	2	2	3	3	2	2	2	1	3	1	3	22
STAFF TREATMENT	1	2	2	3	1	3	3	2	2	3	3	3	3	3	3	3	3	3	3	2	3	3	29
OPENING HRS.	1	1	1	1	1	1	1	1	1	3	2	3	2	1	1	1	1	1	2	1	1	1	12
ATMOSPHERE	2	2	2	2	1	3	3	3	3	3	3	3	3	3	2	3	3	3	2	2	2	2	25
QUAL. OF TREATMENT	3	3	3	3	3	3	3	3	3	3	3	3	3	3	3	3	3	3	3	3	3	3	30
EXT. APPEARANCES	1	1	2	2	1	1	2	2	2	2	2	2	3	2	1	2	1	1	1	1	1	1	14
RANGE OF TREATMENTS	2	2	1	1	1	1	3	2	3	3	3	3	2	1	1	2	1	2	1	2	2	1	14
INTERNAL APPEARANCE	2	2	2	3	2	2	2	3	2	3	2	3	3	2	2	2	2	2	2	1	2	2	20
WAITING TIME	2	3	2	3	3	2	1	2	3	3	3	1	2	3	3	3	1	3	3	1	3	3	25
COMPLIANCE WITH REQUESTS	3	3	3	3	3	3	3	3	3	3	3	3	3	3	2	3	3	3	3	1	3	3	27
CLEANLINESS	3	3	3	3	3	3	3	3	3	3	3	3	3	3	3	3	3	3	3	2	3	3	29

3 = V. IMPORTANT

2 = IMPORTANT

1 = NOT IMPORTANT

DEMAND AT A HAIRDRESSERS

JULIET WELLS

DEMAND FACTORS	23	24	25	26	27	28	29	30	31	32	33	34	35	36	37	38	39	40	TOT.	PART. SCH. TOT.	SCH. TOT.	OVERALL TOT.	
PRICE	3	3	2	2	3	2	2	2	2	1	2	2	1	2	3	1	1	1	35	21	26	82	
LOCATION	3	3	1	2	1	1	2	1	2	3	3	2	2	1	2	1	1	2	33	18	20	71	
REPUTATION	3	3	1	2	2	3	3	2	1	1	3	3	2	2	3	3	3	1	41	22	30	93	
STAFF TREATMENT	3	3	3	2	2	3	3	2	2	2	3	3	3	3	2	3	3	2	47	29	28	104	
OPENING HRS.	1	2	2	1	1	2	1	1	1	1	2	1	1	1	1	1	3	1	24	12	17	58	
ATMOSPHERE	2	2	2	2	1	2	2	1	2	1	3	3	2	2	3	2	3	3	38	25	30	93	
QUAL. OF TREATMENT	3	3	3	3	3	2	1	2	1	2	3	3	3	3	3	3	3	2	46	30	36	112	
EXTERNAL APPEARANCES	2	2	1	2	2	1	2	1	2	2	2	2	2	2	2	1	1	1	30	14	24	65	
RANGE OF TREATMENTS	1	2	1	2	2	2	2	2	1	2	3	3	3	2	2	1	2	1	34	14	25	73	
INTERNAL APPEARANCE	2	2	2	2	3	3	3	3	2	3	2	3	2	2	3	2	3	2	44	20	27	91	
WAITING TIME	3	3	3	3	1	3	1	1	3	1	2	2	1	3	2	1	3	3	39	25	26	90	
COMPLIANCE WITH REQUESTS	3	3	3	3	3	3	3	3	3	3	3	3	3	3	3	3	3	3	54	27	36	117	
CLEANLINESS	3	3	3	3	3	3	3	3	3	3	3	3	3	3	3	3	3	3	54	29	36	119	

INN - TRIM - BIGGEST IN TOWN

3 = VERY IMPORTANT
2 = IMPORTANT
1 = NOT IMPORTANT

INDEX